Pilot Your Life

Pilot Your Life

HOW to CREATE the CAREER YOU WANT

RON SHAW

with

Richard Krevolin

and Phil Ehrenkranz

CINCINNATI, OHIO

Library of Congress Cataloging-in-Publication Data

Shaw, Ron, 1938-
Pilot Your Life : how to create the career you want / Ron Shaw with
Richard Krevolin and Phil Ehrenkranz.
    p. cm.
ISBN 1-57860-185-1
    1. Career development–Handbooks, manuals, etc. 2. Vocational
guidance–Handbooks, manuals, etc. I. Krevolin, Richard W., 1964-
II. Ehrenkranz, Phil. III. Title.
HF5381.S534 2005
650.14–dc22   2004023511

Edited by Jack Heffron
Cover design by Dana Boll and Stephen Sullivan
Interior design by Stephen Sullivan

FOR PHISSY

My inspiration since August 2, 1958

CONTENTS

Foreword

Given that you are reading this foreword, you probably fall into one of two categories: browser or purchaser. Let me explain. The browser is a person who goes to the local bookstore, sometimes with the intention of possibly buying a book and sometimes just to look around or "browse." I frequently fall into this category. I love to read and have been blessed with the good fortune of having a job that allows me to meet and interact with many prolific authors. In the end, many different things affect whether or not I remain a "browser" or become a "purchaser." For instance, I may be drawn to a particular book by something on the book cover. In some cases, it is the title of the book that has garnered my attention; in yet others, it is the author. When I pull the book off of the shelf, I may read the inside jacket cover, the foreword of the book, or the opening lines of the first chapter. Maybe you are doing exactly that right now.

You may have been drawn to this book because you recognized the author on the cover from his humorous commercials for Pilot pens. Perhaps you heard about the book during a recent television interview or read a favorable review. Regardless of how you may have gotten here, you can now consider yourself to be very lucky. Why? Well, first I need to provide you with a bit of background information.

It's hard to believe, but earlier this year I celebrated my forty-fourth anniversary on the air. That means I have now broadcasted on television and radio in six different decades. I broke into the business by starting at a small radio station in Miami Beach on May 1, 1957. I was this little Jewish kid from Brooklyn who dreamed of following in the footsteps of Arthur Godfrey and Red Barber—such giant imprints. I wound up working with both of them at the tail end of their brilliant careers. Early in my career, I actually did radio broadcasts from the window of a delicatessen in Miami Beach (I would tell you more about that here, but the details are contained inside). It was in Miami Beach that I was lucky enough to meet and interview a rising comedian who happened to be a Jewish kid from Philadelphia. Hardly did I know that this aspiring comic would change the path of his life to become the president and CEO of a major pen company. Of course, I am speaking of my friend of over thirty years, Ron Shaw.

When I hear the name Ron Shaw, several adjectives come to mind: honest, compassionate, generous, intelligent, loyal, and, of course, successful. All of these attributes have contributed to Ron becoming one of America's most successful and well-known corporate leaders. Ron is also held in very high regard for his philanthropic goodwill. Ron remains a strong supporter of numerous charitable organizations, including serving as a member of the board of trustees of the charity that I started to help underprivileged individuals pay for life-saving cardiac care: The Larry King Cardiac Foundation. It is in the context of the board meetings of the foundation that I have had the opportunity to observe first-hand and fully appreciate many of the unique and effective methods utilized by Ron in interacting with people. This book will now help you to glean and develop those very same skills.

Pilot Your Life is a delightful journey that offers the reader personal insight into everyday living. This is not an ordinary "how to succeed" guide. This book is what I call a "thoroughly enjoyable read." As you traverse the pages, you will empathize with the various problems and situations that Ron has encountered over the years. You will smile as you read about how he resolves various personal and business dilemmas. The lessons contained in this book are subtle and effective; incidentally, these are two other adjectives that are aptly used to describe the author.

In this day and age, we frequently hear about what some people refer to as the "ruthless corporate ethic" in American business. That type of perception seems to support the old cliché that "nice guys finish last." In this book, Ron Shaw completely debunks that theory. He proves that with hard work, your own initiative, and the common sense plainly laid out in the following pages, you can not only succeed in your personal and professional life, but that you can enjoy yourself, family, and friends while in the process of doing so.

At this point, if you are still a "browser," you have now come to the time to make an important decision: Do I put the book back on the shelf, or do I buy it? If you make the right choice, I am confident that you will have absolutely no regrets. If you have already purchased *Pilot Your Life*, congratulations. You are about to embark upon a fun and hopefully life-changing flight.

Larry King

Acknowledgments

As a CEO appearing in TV commercials and media interviews, I sometimes find myself in the awkward position of getting undeserved credit for single-handedly building Pilot Pen Corporation of America's operation; in fact, there are hundreds of people who have been responsible for Pilot Pen's past and present success. I cannot list all of them here, but I strongly believe that any executive who has been made to "look good" must, of necessity, have an excellent top management team reporting to him or her, and I am no exception.

Those who deserve special recognition and thanks for having been essential to our company are: Greg Bohnsack, Dennis Burleigh, Laurie Faulkner, Joe Kiewlen, Jim Plunkett, Tom Restivo, Bob Silberman, and Patty Skarupa.

None of the work would have any satisfaction if it weren't for my family. Special thanks to my wife, Phyllis Shaw, and children, Steve Shaw, Susan Shaw Santoro, and Alan Shaw, for their tolerance of my travel schedule and late hours over the years, as well as their support and encouragement for my writing this book.

My deep appreciation also goes to Richard Krevolin, whose vision, tenacity, and talent brought this book to life. In addition, I thank the following for their immeasurable help in putting this book together: Irwin Helford, Larry King, Sherman Krevolin, Murray and Marvin Lender, Harvey Mackay, Jack Paige, Peter Rubie, Michael Santoro, Carrie Shaw, Nancy Shaw, Shana Smith, Tom Stemberg, tireless agent June Rifkin Clark, and editor Jack Heffron.

Finally, special thanks go to Phil Ehrenkranz, one of my boyhood buddies throughout my childhood in Miami. When we were kids, Phil wanted to be a reporter while I was already working in show business. He made me promise that when we grew up, he'd be the one to write the book about my exciting climb to comedic fame. My show business career never met his high expectations, however, and Phil became an attorney instead of a reporter. Nevertheless, he has been a tremendous help in shaping these words.

Introduction

I'm into the home stretch of my comedy act and the audience is with me all the way, leaning toward me in their seats, laughing and erupting into applause so often that I need to allow extra time before I tell my next joke. It's one of the greatest feelings in the world; a rush I experienced onstage for eleven years, from the time I was a kid of eleven to a newly married twenty-two-year-old man.

However, as a new husband with responsibilities, I suddenly needed to get a steady job. Yet my only training was as a comedian. Little did I know that my onstage education would help me beat the odds and become a successful CEO.

At the time I had no idea spending my youth in the spotlight had any applications beyond the stage, but now I see in retrospect that comedy and business have a great deal in common. Many of the lessons I learned as a comedian have been instrumental to my success over the course of my business career (and even saved my behind a few times). In addition, I came to realize that the seemingly innocuous jokes I used to tell onstage are metaphors for what's important in business and in life.

Is there a secret to success? After working as a comedian, then a salesman, and ultimately the president and CEO of Pilot Pen Corporation of America, I have learned there is one essential secret to success in business and in life. This secret applies to just about every successful CEO, gutsy entrepreneur, and each fulfilled person I've met.

The secret is: never wait for someone else to give you permission to pursue your dreams.

Just as the sun doesn't wait for permission to rise and the stars appear without waiting for their cue, you can go after the life you want without needing permission.

Follow your passions! Allow yourself to be bold! Of course, you must act within the law and uphold moral and ethical standards. But knowing this secret is the first step in seizing the controls of your life.

"Okay," you say, "but first I need a job." Among other things, this book is meant to persuade you that once you accept that you're the one who's in charge of making the most of your life, you're on your way to a fulfilling career, and not just a job to pay the bills. Whether the direction you want to go is starting your own company or eventually running a business, you'll need to develop and master certain capabilities: vision, goals, strategy, focus, hard work, concern for other people, attention to detail and quality, delegation of responsibility, resilience, and then a little more hard work. You'll need to recognize the difference between risky and reckless. Most of all, you'll have to pay attention to the lessons life throws in your path, then apply that hard-won knowledge to the next challenge.

Obviously, no one starting out can acquire these abilities before making a career decision. They are learned on the job, whether you have no business school education or an MBA. So where do you begin? Because I had the advantage of a first career in stand-up comedy "selling" jokes to live audiences, it was a natural transition for me to sell products to live customers. Even though chances are fairly good you don't have a performing-on-stage background, you still should consider sales as your takeoff point for a business career.

To explain this advice, let's look at the basics. Every business has at least three major parts: (1) the substantive (manufacturing, technical or creative) functions, (2) sales, and (3) executive (administrative and management) functions. Although attaining success in the latter two categories requires intimate knowledge of the first, my experience, and therefore the focus of this book, is on sales and management. If you have sales success, you likely will be given supervisory responsibilities (as a sales manager, for example) and move "up" to management, as I did. I purposely placed quotes around "up" because even in management, you never truly leave sales; nor should you, because selling is at the core of every business. Your business can have great technical innovators and fine administrators, but unless your product or service is sold, there will be little or nothing to refine or manage. I don't mean here to unduly minimize the importance of the substantive and administrative aspects, as no business can flourish unless all three parts work harmoniously. Indeed, my job as CEO is to manage the company. It's just my strong belief that selling is at the heart of the enterprise—and, as you can tell, first in my business heart as well.

Furthermore, especially for those who are not fortified with an institutional business education, but even for some who are, sales provides a readily available entry into the business world; and since the usual progression of a successful salesperson is into management, a sales career affords a good opportunity for upward mobility. In my opinion, the lessons learned at the heart of the business result in the best salespeople becoming the best managers. Over the course of a forty-three year career, I learned (most of) those lessons, and you can too, if you'll just read on.

So you want to rise to the very top—to occupy the CEO chair. But do you have a clear idea of what awaits you there? Probably not. It's always intrigued me how young people choose careers without knowing much about what really will occupy their workdays. For better or worse, the TV shows *Perry Mason* and *Law & Order* inspired many law careers, and *ER*, many medical careers. But there's not much on television about the business life of a CEO. Even *The Apprentice*, starring Donald Trump, doesn't allow the viewer to look over The Donald's shoulder as he conducts his business ventures. Another purpose of this book, therefore, is to give you some idea of what senior executives, particularly CEOs, actually do in their jobs. If those of you just starting out don't know what's involved in being a CEO, how could you know you want to be one, let alone believe you could do the job well?

In the course of giving you such job descriptions, any time I advise you "as an executive," keep in mind that I'm not suggesting you must achieve managerial status before that advice is meaningful to you. It's my main intention in those instances to let you in on the types of situations business executives encounter and how they deal with them. You don't have to learn now, for example, how to make personnel decisions, structure a sales force, conduct public relations and advertising campaigns, or engage in legal dispute resolution. But just being fortified with the knowledge that these are the kinds of tasks business executives undertake, should more fully inform your choices about what you ultimately hope to achieve in a lifetime career.

When my adult children learned about the idea for this book, they said "Great!" and "We want to tell your readers that following your advice leads to success." So that I can continue to be included in family gatherings, here are their comments to you.

* * *

During our family dinners (when Dad wasn't traveling), we'd hear about his day at work intermingled with jokes and general fun. It was a great way to learn of the world and business in general. As a family where everyone had something to say, I learned when to speak my thoughts and when to hold back. I also learned to listen and to respect others. Now I realize that I was learning to be a successful person, a successful husband and bread-winner, and most importantly a successful dad. Some of the key business traits I learned from my father are:

❖ To appreciate, from a very young age, the value of money and how it affects (positively and negatively) so many people.

❖ To think of the mental, physical, and financial benefits of working for yourself.

❖ To understand how people view you by the way you comb your hair, wear your clothes, tie your tie, and polish your shoes.

❖ To learn the power of language, good grammar, and written and verbal communication.

❖ To learn that self-confidence is one of the easiest and most important traits to acquire.

❖ To sell yourself.

❖ To help your children create their own meaning or success in business and life.

—*Alan Shaw*

* * *

Dad taught me that no star is out of reach; that if I want something, I should go after it. His encouragement gave me the daring to think big and reach for those stars. As a real estate agent, I work by "if you want the order, ask for it" every day. Dad's stories about working with customers at Bic and Pilot, and how he learned to listen to them instead of jumping into a sales pitch, taught me to focus on making friends instead of just getting customers.

—*Susan Shaw Santor*

* * *

My father is a guy who says what he's going to do, then does what he says. I guess that reads as planning your work, and working your plan. About the only word of advice he ever gave me that he didn't follow himself was, "Go into business for yourself." I did. He didn't. One time a reporter asked me, "Who is your hero?" Without hesitation (and never having given a thought to personal heroes) I said, "My dad." The reasons why are in this book.

—*Steve Shaw*

* * *

This book isn't filled with hype and hyperbole. It's a series of personal stories and humorous tales from my years in show business and the pen business, each intended to provide lessons and instructive insights so you can be spared some of the anguish and embarrassment I endured. I hope that you'll experience much of the exhilaration without a good deal of the exasperation as you successfully *Pilot Your Life.*

—*Ron Shaw*

President and CEO

Pilot Pen Corporation of America

Trumbull, Connecticut

1

Potential Disasters
Are Your Friends

One evening when I was on the road, I was staying at the Concord Hotel in the Catskill Mountains. It was late at night and I was desperately trying to get some sleep before my big show the next day. I was in bed about to nod off when suddenly I heard this conversation coming from the next room.

A man was saying, "Darling, you've got an incredible face. When we get back to Philadelphia, I'm going to hire one of those chiseler guys to sculpt your face in stone."

I tried not to listen and turned over in bed. Then I heard, "And you've got the most beautiful body I've ever seen. When we get back to Philadelphia, I'm going to have that chiseler guy chisel your body in stone, too."

Things were starting to sound interesting now, so I put my ear up against the wall to listen in. "Oh honey, you've got the most perfect, beautiful breasts in the world. When we get back to Philadelphia, I'm going to have them chiseled in stone."

I couldn't take it anymore, so I put on my robe, went out in the hall, and knocked on my neighbor's door. The guy inside yelled, "Who's there?"

I answered, "The chiseler from Philadelphia!"

That was one of my favorite jokes. It never failed to get a laugh, and I have told it hundreds of times over the years. Like many things in my professional lives, I stayed with it as long as it worked. But let me explain how I went from professional teenage joke teller to "slightly" older man making his living as President of a leading pen company. There is no better place to begin than the beginning.

I never met the chiseler, but "opened" on September 17, 1938 in the City of Brotherly Love, the birthplace of our nation, Philadelphia, Pennsylvania, where I was born to Herb and Babe Schurowitz. Two and a half years later, my little sister, Rachel, was born, and our family was complete. My father was a driver/salesman for the Baldwin Uniform Company. In our apartment in the Mayfair section of Philadelphia, we had an old upright piano that my mother loved to play. She was quite a talented classical pianist. As a child, I always loved to listen to her play.

Then one day when I was six, I heard the song "Don't Fence Me In" on the radio. I liked the way it sounded so much, I sat down at the piano, my feet swinging above the floor, and started picking out my own rendition of the melody with one finger—pretty poorly, mind you, but I could replay it fairly well. When my mother realized what I had just done, she screamed with delight and was instantly convinced that she had given birth to the next Mozart or at least George Gershwin. Immediately, she decided to invest what little extra money our family had in piano lessons to foster my burgeoning musical talent.

But nobody in Philadelphia wanted to give piano lessons to a six-year-old kid. They all assumed that within a few months I would, like most other young boys, move on to other interests and drop my lessons. Fortunately, my mother wouldn't give up and finally found a wonderful teacher by the name of Earl Moyer. Mr. Moyer led an orchestra at the Adelphi Hotel by night and gave piano lessons during the day. Like all the other teachers, he too was reluctant; but my mother's relentless entreating finally compelled him to take me on. Mr. Moyer turned out to be my only music teacher, and I've enjoyed playing piano ever since.

Looking back, I realize I would never have been able to enter show business if my mother hadn't persisted in finding a piano teacher for me. Even though everyone told her that she'd never find someone willing to instruct a six-year-old, she refused to listen and kept pushing. My mom provided me with piano instruction— and my first lesson in the value of perseverance.

Besides our piano, the other things I remember most clearly about Philadelphia were the frigid winters, the hard black ice on the streets, and the brutal, freezing winds.

Let me take you back to the streets of Philly during the winter of 1947. The war had been over for two years. We were knee-deep in the American Century and the United States had proven itself the new leader of the world. Things were looking up. There was a sense of potential and expectation in the air. Anything could happen.

We had moved from the Mayfair section of Philadelphia to the Germantown section because, during a driver's strike in 1946 at the company where my dad worked, my mother convinced him to get out of the uniform delivery business and buy a candy store. They used their life savings to buy a little shop on the corner of Chelton Avenue and Anderson Street. Our store had a soda fountain and a big glass candy counter. We also sold over-the-counter medicines like aspirin and cough syrup.

I was literally a kid in a candy store. Our family lived in an apartment above the store. My father also worked out of the store as the local bookie. He was able to make a nice living and things were looking up for our family. But that was about to change. We were one of just a few Jewish families in our section of German-town. Late one night, bricks and rocks crashed through our plate glass window with notes attached that read "Jews not welcome!" and "Jew go home!" The midnight "hate mail" continued on and off for months.

My mother came down with a nervous skin condition because of the onslaught of anti-Semitism. It was hard on all of us. As a scrawny little Jewish kid trying to get home from school in one piece, occasionally I had to fight larger boys who bullied me and pushed me around. One afternoon a gang of rowdies threw me down into an open sewer.

A few months later, on a day permanently etched in my memory, I was walking quickly and silently down Chelton Avenue, trying to avoid trouble. In a way, it was a serene and beautiful winter day; the streets were quiet and almost devoid of people and cars since the roads were so icy. But I was a Jewish kid walking through a predominantly Gentile neighborhood in the late 1940s —even on this quiet winter day I felt anything but safe and serene. Yet I had no choice: It was getting late and I had to get home. So I walked as fast as I could, and I almost made it. Just a few blocks from our store, the silence was shattered by the words "Rotten Jew! Kike! Dirty Jew bastard!" The toughs who had thrown me down the sewer suddenly reappeared. I was surrounded by four boys, all of them bigger. I desperately looked around, hoping that someone might recognize what was about to happen and come to my aid, but unfortunately the weather was so bad that all the good-hearted, sane people were safe and warm indoors.

I was no coward. Sure, I was scared, but I was one of those skinny boys who wanted the world to believe that I was a lot more physically intimidating than I looked. Of course, no one ever fell for my bluffing, but I kept it up all the same. You see, in those days in our neighborhood, you couldn't easily back down from a fight. Well, to be honest, I'm not really sure if you could or not; my tormentors and I never really paused to discuss street fight protocol. What mattered was that I was a Jewish kid, and since these were not politically correct Gentile boys, I was in for a hell of a beating.

I tried my best to fight back, managing to stay on my feet long enough to withstand a few blows to my stomach and a right hook to the eye. I even got in a few good punches myself, but before I knew it, I was down on the sidewalk. Suddenly, a hand grabbed me by the neck and lifted me up. I was going to be saved. Hallelujah! Unfortunately, the hand belonged to one of the bigger kids, who cursed at me and held me with my arms behind my back

25

as a trolley car sped towards us. At the very last second, he spun me out onto the street and pushed me in front of the trolley.

Hitting the ground with a thud, I instantly looked up and saw the huge steel streetcar heading straight toward me. I tried to move, to get out of the way, to get onto my feet, but I couldn't. I was skidding across the ice too quickly and slid all the way across a slick patch of black ice on the street, just as the trolley car whizzed past my head.

It missed me by inches, literally inches. Talk about your life-altering incidents. I'll never be able to forget that moment. I don't know if God meant for me to live because there was work he wanted me to do or if it was just a fluke that a patch of black ice happened to be on the street at that spot, but somehow, for whatever reason, I survived.

As I skidded across Chelton Avenue, I had a revelation of the gift of life I had been given. Since then, I have grasped the irony that I was saved by slipping: I hated cold and ice, but if it hadn't been for those cold, icy conditions that winter day, I'd be dead instead of writing this book.

As you will see, my life and career were punctuated by other opportunities to rebound from adversity. Being broke was one. Getting fired was another. Making occasional poor business decisions were still others. Yet from those crises came knowledge that led to prosperity. Belief in yourself and your ability to realize your ambitions is the foundation for the courage that will allow you not just to withstand setbacks, but to gain something from each of them.

2

Innovate, Negotiate, Succeed

Looking for a human-interest story, a reporter for a Miami paper approached three mature gentlemen sitting on a bench. The reporter asked, "What do you do all day?"

The first mature gentleman said, "I don't do anything." The second mature gentleman said, "Neither do I." The third mature gentleman said, "What a question! Look at this beautiful place. Look at the cloudless sky, the shining sun, the warm air, and nature giving us every bounty."

The reporter said, "But what do you do all day?"

The third mature gentleman said, "I help them!"

Soon after the trolley car incident, my mother's skin condition became nearly unbearable. Her rashes grew so bad on her hands and feet that she thought she had skin cancer. Her condition was exacerbated by the cold weather and her close proximity to the ice cream freezers in our store. She was suffering and something had to change.

Her doctor recommended that we move to a warmer climate. "Either Arizona or Florida," he suggested. In those days, there were very few Jews in Arizona, so we opted for Florida. My father sold the store and we took a train down to Miami. We arrived on Mother's Day, 1948, and my cold Philly days gave way to warm Miami nights. I was nine and a half.

My father decided to open a dry-cleaning store in Miami with a man named Harry, who happened to be a total stranger recommended to us by a distant relative. Since my dad's name is Herb and his partner's was Harry, they decided to call themselves H & H Cleaners. Soon after they opened their store, however, cash started disappearing, and then Harry disappeared.

Only six months after arriving in Miami, my dad had lost his store and his life savings, and he was forced to support us by selling peanuts and popcorn in the grandstands of the Orange Bowl. It was a tough time for all of us. My mother, who was a registered nurse, helped out by working in doctors' offices and the Miami Jewish Home for the Aged. Fortunately, in a few months my father was able to get a job driving a laundry truck just like he had years earlier in Philadelphia. But my father's dream of succeeding with his own business was gone with Harry.

In retrospect, it's easy to say that Harry was no good, but at the time, it seemed reasonable to rely on our relative's favorable recommendation of Harry and on Harry's trustworthy appearance. Unfortunately, by the time my father discovered who and what Harry really was, he had departed with all of my father's money. This left a lasting impression on me: Don't accept something on face value; find out the background and credentials of all parties involved before committing yourself.

Even though things were rough for our family when we first moved south, Miami was my kind of town and I took to it very quickly. No snow; palm trees everywhere; clean, sandy beaches; and lots of great restaurants and theaters—what was not to like?

Thanks to Harry, though, our family had little money. So, I did what any good-hearted, red-blooded American kid would do—I applied for a paper route. There were only two requirements for having a paper route. You had to be twelve years old, and you had to have your own bike. I didn't have a bike, so my father went down to the police auction and got a beat-up bicycle for me for only five dollars. I was ready for my first job.

With a bike, I felt confident that I could get the job—even

though I was only ten. When I got down to the office to apply, there was one other kid applying to be a paperboy, Arnie Swedler. He too was only ten. Arnie and I discussed our predicament. We both decided to become two years older that day, and as a result, we both were awarded routes in our neighborhoods. The ambition Arnie and I showed in that office was to characterize both our business careers. As an adult, Arnie moved from Florida to Canada. Learning that there was pent-up demand in Ottawa for deli foods like pickled herring, pastrami, and corned beef, he opened a wholesale food business there catering to supermarkets. He has since opened Arnie's, a wholesale food company serving restaurants and take-out delis. He has done extremely well for himself.

Every day, I got on my beat-up bike and delivered my papers. I knew that if I worked hard all week and conscientiously delivered every single copy of The Miami Daily News entrusted to me, I would be able to make about twelve dollars a week. This seemed like a lot of money to me then and would have kept me happy if I didn't happen to walk past the storefront window of Harry's Bike Shop (no relation to the Harry on the lam). You see, featured in Harry's window was a thing of rare beauty. Yep, I was smitten, not by a girl, but a Schwinn Black Phantom bicycle. Cushy leather seat, sleek black and red frame, wide handlebars— I had to have it, especially before any of the other kids got one.

The only problem was that the new bicycle cost eighty-six dollars that I didn't have. I tried not to think about it, but all day long all I could think about was riding my route atop that beautiful Black Phantom. I would be the envy of every kid in Miami. But with my paper route income, I knew it would be months before I'd be able to afford that bike.

Still, I couldn't wait. I had to have it—right then and there! So, I decided to try negotiating with Harry and went down to the bike shop. No one had told me how to talk to Harry or offered me advice on how to negotiate a deal. I just thought I'd give it a shot and see what I could do. I walked into the shop and approached Harry with a proposal. I told him that I had six dollars in my pocket that I would give him as a down payment, and I would sign a piece of paper guaranteeing him five dollars a week until the bike was paid in full.

Harry chuckled at first, presumably at my audacity, but soon my serious demeanor made him consider my proposal. I was adamant, and even though I was only ten, he could tell I meant business. And wouldn't you know it, Harry accepted my proposal and handed me my very own Schwinn Black Phantom bicycle. I was in heaven riding it home from the shop. And for the next sixteen weeks, I made every five-dollar payment to Harry until my debt was paid off—interest-free at that. Just as my mom wouldn't accept failing to find a piano teacher for me, so I wouldn't accept not riding that Black Phantom out of that store that day. It was one of many lessons I've learned about the persuasive power of conviction, perseverance and passion—and an offer that was innovative and, for that time, unconventional.

Sure, buying on credit, though rare, wasn't unknown in the late 1940s, but Harry the business owner hadn't thought of it as a way to make a sale. And truthfully, even if he had, I don't think we would have made a deal but for the determination I exhibited.

This kid-gets-bike tale was an early triumph that entitles me to a little repetition for emphasis. Bring to your business endeavors what I summoned that day: Conviction. Perseverance. Passion. Innovation. Determination.

(Quick note: In the mid-1990s, Schwinn released a limited-edition remake of the Black Phantom, and again, I felt like I had to have one. Though the price was a few thousand dollars, this time I was able to purchase one without negotiating an installment plan. And so today, more than fifty years later, I am once again the proud owner of a beautiful Schwinn Black Phantom bicycle.)

3

Risk Is the Handmaiden
of Opportunity

I won't say he's a lush...but this guy drinks like Johnnie Walker needs his bottles back.

That borrowed one-liner was among the jokes I told the first time I stood on stage and delivered a comedy routine. It also represents my first career transition: paperboy to comedian.

My paper route was a great way to make money, but it wasn't enough for me. I wanted more. I wanted to be in the spotlight, making music, performing.

At the time, south Florida was the place to be for an aspiring performer. You have to understand that Miami in the late forties and early fifties was like Las Vegas or Atlantic City today—where all the great performers and musicians wanted to be. The city had fantastic nightclubs, both free-standing and inside the numerous luxury hotels. Performing was in the air.

Each day, several paperboys and I would sit on a curb in front of an empty lot to fold and rubber band our papers for delivery. We'd race to see who could complete his route first, but I'd always lose on Fridays. I'd stay behind to read the "Youth Round-Up" section, two pages of articles from local junior high and high schools, plus a story about a weekly radio show also called *Youth Round-Up.*

Owned by The Miami Daily News, the radio show was taped every Saturday afternoon downtown in The News Tower (now known as the Freedom Tower) and aired during prime time on Monday nights by the NBC affiliate WIOD. It was sponsored by Coca-Cola and featured teenage talent. In every show, young singers and musicians performed, young people discussed problems they faced in life, and then one of the teenage cast members interviewed a major star of the day, like Clark Gable, Eddie Cantor, Patti Page, Jimmy Durante, or Nat King Cole.

I listened to the show each Monday evening, then eagerly read about it in the Friday paper. It seemed like the kids on the show had a lot of fun and I began wondering if I could get on by playing the piano.

In July 1950, after a year-and-a-half of fantasizing about performing on the show, I took a bus to the station and asked if I could audition. I was eleven-and-a-half. I played the tango song "La Cumparsita." I was praying just to be one of the guest musicians when the producer, Dave Rabinowitz, told me that he liked my piano playing. When I thanked him, he also said it sounded like my voice was right for radio and he offered me a role as a regular member of the cast. I was overjoyed. I had walked in hoping to get on the show once, for just a few minutes, and I left as a regular cast member who appeared weekly for the next thirty-six months.

On the show each week, I went out into the studio audience and picked contestants at random for the "Quizeroo." Players had to identify either the name or composer of certain musical interludes.

During this time, after my thirteenth birthday, I was fortunate to watch the incredible performances of two musical talents, Buddy Rich and Rosemary Clooney, on stage at the Olympia Theater. Buddy was already a famous jazz drummer, but Rosemary was still a relatively unknown vocalist who had just been signed by Columbia Records. Rosemary came to our radio station for an interview, and she and I struck up a conversation. With her singing talent, personality, and beauty, I knew she was something special. I was only thirteen, Jewish, and still waiting for my growth spurt, and

Rosemary was twenty-three, Irish-Catholic, and on the brink of fame. We couldn't have been more different, but we formed a friendship that continued until she died in 2002. I became her most ardent fan, formed a Rosemary Clooney fan club, and thereby received a stack of her records. Every night, I would visit disc jockeys at radio stations all over Miami and beg, plead, and cajole them to play her newest single.

Rosemary had no idea what I was doing and, when she found out, urged me to stop. I agreed, but I was so passionate about her singing that I wanted to share it with the world. Rosemary said I was the most outgoing kid she ever met. But I never saw myself as really outgoing. In essence, I guess I've always had the sales gene. Whether it was pushing Rosemary Clooney records or jokes, I couldn't help myself. When I believe in a product, I do everything I can to make it succeed.

In 1953, when I was fourteen, I was still appearing on *Youth Round-Up*. Our ratings took a nosedive because television shows were drawing off the radio audience. The show's coordinator, Betty Ward, pushed to repackage us as a television program, and we were picked up for broadcast by a local TV station. Unfortunately, what was fantastic on radio turned out to be horrible on TV, and we were canceled after only thirteen weeks.

But Betty still believed in us and put us together as a performing unit for military personnel stationed throughout Florida. We were known as the "Youth Round-Up Stars on Parade." Basically, she took all the regular teenage cast members and put us on stage as a sort of USO (United Service Organizations) type of show that could play for servicemen anywhere around the state. It was a great thrill for us kids to have a chance to perform for appreciative military audiences in those spacious, well-equipped, military-base theaters.

At this point in my career, I only played piano. However, after awhile, Betty asked me to introduce the acts because she thought my radio experience would lend itself to being a master of ceremony. I enjoyed emceeing and tickling the ivories, but found that what I loved most was watching our group's comedian perform. I was fascinated by the way he moved his hands when he told jokes, how he held the microphone, how he walked, and how he timed his punch lines. I wanted to know everything about the way he worked.

After a couple of months, I'd seen him do his routine so many times I knew every one of his lines by heart. It wasn't exactly a conscious thing; it was more like osmosis. His act seeped into me, and I never really thought about what I had learned until one night when he didn't show up to perform.

It was five minutes before we were supposed to start and Betty was terribly upset. More than one thousand GIs had come to see our show and we didn't have a comic. She pulled me aside and said, "Okay, Ronnie, can you do it?"

I didn't want to let Betty down, and since I knew his act cold, I agreed. Thank God I knew his whole routine so well, because when I stepped out on that stage, I could not think. Hell, I could barely move! There I was, a fifteen-year-old kid in the spotlight in front of hundreds of GIs, trying to make them laugh. I was a nervous wreck!

I remember that long walk up to the microphone with that white-hot spotlight on me, the whole time convinced that my legs were going to buckle or I'd have a heart attack. I'd played piano for lots of different people and never got nervous, but comedy, I found that night, is a different ballgame altogether. It's like being naked up there. And if you don't hook the audience quickly, you're dead. Even if you do grab them, you can lose them in any given second with one bad punch line. It's a tenuous thing and you've got to hold on tight, which is hard as hell when you're suffering from a horrible case of stage fright.

Not knowing what else to do, I cleared my throat and just started blabbering.....I told the Johnnie Walker one-liner and all the jokes I'd heard the regular comic say show after show and,

37

miraculously, the GIs erupted into uncontrollable laughter. Every laugh made it that much easier. Soon I relaxed and was loving it. In comedy, momentum is everything.

That night I learned that even if you're scared to death, you can't show weakness or vulnerability. Your audience will sense it and be uneasy with you. Fortunately, I had studied the details of our comedian's performances so thoroughly, not only could I deliver his jokes, but I also unconsciously mimicked his confident stance and mannerisms. Like an emergency service worker or soldier, I responded the way I was trained—even though I never realized I was training myself.

When you are in the spotlight, you have to make it appear as if you're relaxed, even if you're not, so that your audience can relax in your presence. It's a reciprocal thing. And then, when both the audience and you feel comfortable, wondrous things can happen. Laughter pours forth, and it's one of the greatest rushes in the world. You have power. Control. Immortality, it seems. You are the life of the party. No other feeling is quite like it.

It was years later that I recognized how profoundly this period of my life shaped my future. That kid who got around an age requirement to get a paper route, convinced a store owner to accept a payment plan on a new bicycle, won a three-year role on a radio show, promoted Rosemary Clooney records to nightshift DJs, and walked onstage to tell borrowed jokes in front of hundreds of servicemen taught me the value of taking risks, being innovative and inventive, following passions, and, most of all, not waiting for someone else to give me permission to pursue what I wanted. That kid taught me about recognizing and seizing opportunities to improve skills, expand talent, and foster the ability to sell myself, and about how relaxing and enjoying myself helps an audience (or customers) relax and enjoy themselves. That kid taught me the importance of momentum in the process of selling jokes, ideas, myself—and pens.

The day I became a comedian I had five minutes, not exactly sufficient time for extensive analysis, to decide whether I would risk my self-esteem and seize the opportunity to perform. When opportunities suddenly present themselves, don't automatically back off just because they're sudden, and don't be afraid of being afraid. That's just natural. Your mind, your instincts and your heart will tell you whether you're ready to assume the risks involved and try to succeed despite your fears. If they tell you yes, you are ready, then go for it, because there is no timetable for opportunity.

4

Reinvent Yourself

A young writer brought a manuscript into a publisher. The publisher said, "We only publish books by authors with well-known names."
The writer said, "Terrific! My name is Smith!"

That first night I stood on stage as a comedian was the second unforgettable moment in my life. There I was, Ronald Schurowitz, not exactly a well-known name, a mere fifteen-year-old, doing my first comedy performance, and I had those GIs convinced I was the funniest guy they'd ever met. Now let me tell you, for a teenager, this was heady stuff. I'm talking a standing ovation, the whole nine yards. Betty was elated with my performance, and I never played piano for her again. I was now officially a comedian!

Obviously, I loved comedy. My parents, on the other hand, weren't so sure about it, but I used the money I was making to help pay for my college education. You have to understand that my parents were not showbiz people. Though they wanted the best for me, as second-generation American children of immigrants, there was little precedent for this kind of strange behavior in my family. Neither my mother nor father had ever been on stage. True, I had one cousin, Arne Sultan, who was a record mimic (he did a form of lip-synching to records which is rarely seen today) and who went on to become a TV producer and writer for The *Judy Garland Show* and *Get Smart*. But in general we were not a family of entertainers.

Yet, for whatever reason, I was always drawn to performing. For eleven years, being on stage was my life. I think there's something to the adage that once stage performing gets in your blood, it never goes away. I guess that's why I still enjoy talking about it, and maybe that's why I still pay my dues to two theatrical unions—AGVA (American Guild of Variety Artists, the nightclub performers' union) and the Musician's Federation.

When I was sixteen and had been doing comedy for about a year, I thought I might jump-start my career by changing my name from Ronald Schurowitz to something that would be a little easier to pronounce. The only hitch was that I had received a small fourteen-karat gold ring from my parents for my Bar Mitzvah with the initials RS on it. I didn't want to have to stop wearing it on stage; so I limited myself to picking a new last name that started with S. Actually, Ronald Smith would have qualified. But at the time, publishing a book was not on my mind, and my great-uncle Sam Bernstein suggested Shaw, and I liked the way it sounded.

"SHAW!"

It rolls off the tongue with grace and ease. So, that's how I became—Ronnie Shaw!

A few years later, I had to change my name once again—but this time it was only for three weeks. Here's what happened.

In the thirties and forties, there was a famous nightclub in New York City on 52nd Street called Leon and Eddie's. It was a launching pad for many of the greatest comedians of that time. Jackie Gleason, Phil Silvers, Alan King, and many others played there. When one of the owners, Leon Enken, retired to Florida in the 1950s, he opened Leon and Eddie's as a strip joint in what is now called the South Beach part of Miami Beach. This new club was a direct descendant of the old-time burlesque houses that featured five strippers, a comedian, a novelty act, and a three-piece band. It was a large club, and anything but a classy place.

One day I got a call from Leon's club. They offered me $125

to perform as a comedian for one week. At that time, I wasn't working and I couldn't afford to say no, though I really didn't want to be associated with that type of establishment. Although $125 sounded like a lot of money back then, it wasn't exactly an easy payday. Leon expected me to perform in three shows a night, seven nights a week.

I agreed to work there on condition that I perform under a name other than Ronnie Shaw. In keeping with this request, I stipulated that Leon wasn't allowed to use my picture in any ads that might run in the papers or on any signs outside the club. Leon didn't have any problem with those conditions, so I signed a contract.

As I approached the club on opening night, I was taken aback. A big sign in front of the club announced, "America's newest comedy sensation—Rod Roberts."

Yep, Leon had kept his part of the bargain and kept my name and photo off the marquee, and instead, he had renamed me— Rod Roberts. Not the most distinctive name in the world (apologies to all the real Rod Robertses), but it would work. I laughed and went inside.

I worked hard all week doing my twenty-one shows, and on closing night, big Leon walked over to me. I looked at him. Weighing in at over two hundred fifty pounds, a long stogie hanging from his lower lip, he sat down next to me and said, in his distinctively low husky growl, "Kid, you're great. We want to hold you over."

Now, to a novice in the comedy world, this might sound fantastic. But if you've been around a little, you know that as soon as you hear those words you are about to be suckered into a ploy used by club owners who don't have enough money to pay you. I called him on it. "So basically what you're saying to me, Leon, is you don't have my one hundred twenty-five dollars, right?"

Leon blew some cigar smoke in my face and said, "Nahh. That's not it at all. You're great. GREAT!" He slipped me fifty dollars. "Here's fifty bucks against the one-twenty-five I owe you."

I reluctantly took the fifty. I needed it and I knew that I could continue to argue with him all night, but I wasn't going to get another red cent out of him. I nodded and grunted, "All right, Leon, one more week, and at the end of that, I want all my money for both weeks, okay?"

"Sure kid. Anything you say."

He blew another puff of smoke in my face and lumbered away. Of course, at the end of the next week, Leon only paid me the balance of the first week, and nothing for the second week. So, now, I'd worked for him for two weeks—forty-two shows—and I only had $125 to show for it.

Of course, when I confronted Leon about it, he smiled and said, "Kid, you're the best. I like you." He should have liked me, since he was hardly paying me. Then he said, "I don't normally do this, but I'm gonna bring you back for another week. How 'bout that?"

"Okay, Leon. FINE! One more week. But I want all my money by the end of the week, okay? That's two hundred fifty dollars next week. OKAY?"

"Sure, you got it. All of it. I promise." I knew the game he was playing with me, but I reluctantly agreed. I really wanted to get my money from him.

And so, one week later, after twenty-one consecutive nights and sixty-three shows, when I walked up to Leon and asked for my money, wouldn't you know it, he looked at me and said, "Kid, you're the king of comedy. Unfortunately, I'm a little low on funds right now. How 'bout you work just one more week and I promise, I'll definitely have all your money by then. I swear!"

"That's it! No thanks!" I said as I quit and walked out of that crummy place. The next morning, I went to the union, told them my story, and showed them the contract. They went after Leon, and within a week, I received all of my money.

And that, my friends, was the beginning and the end of the career of America's newest comedy sensation, Rod Roberts.

Did I learn anything from this incarnation? I sure did. I learned that handshake agreements are unreliable; get your agreement in writing. I learned that when you need money but don't want to risk your reputation, you may want to reinvent yourself with a new name. Even if you don't have much use for a new incarnation, stand up for yourself, and use what leverage you have when more polite means of resolving a dispute have been exhausted.

5

First Impressions
Can Be Deceiving

I was very fortunate to play in many clubs and hotels in Miami that featured some of the hottest comedians and singers in the country. I even had a tiny role in the Jerry Lewis film *The Bellboy*, but unfortunately my scene was cut.

After I started making some headway as a comedian, I was asked to do a radio interview. I agreed until I found out I was to be interviewed in a deli—which meant the interview was for the late-night *Larry King Show*.

I'd heard Larry's show before and didn't really know what to make of it. So I told the press agent, "I'm not sure. Anyone who does his radio show from a deli is going nowhere in show business!"

Reluctantly, I finally agreed to do the interview and went over to Pumpernik's. Maybe at least I'd get a free pastrami sandwich out of it.

When Larry interviewed me, I had to sit on a little stage near the front window. I remember thinking to myself that he seemed like a nice guy, but with that gravelly voice, how could he expect to make it in radio? It just goes to show (again) that first impressions can be highly deceiving.

As most everyone knows, Larry went on to do incredibly well in a very competitive industry. Larry came from humble origins, and his success story is wonderfully instructive. As a boy named Larry Zeiger growing up in New York, he became fascinated by radio at age five. He remembers spending much of his youth pretending to be a radio announcer. He was a good student and a happy kid until his father, a Russian immigrant who worked in a defense plant building ships, died of a heart attack when Larry was just nine. Larry took his father's death hard and lost interest in school. Without his father's income to help support their family, his mother, a seamstress, had to apply for relief—what we now call welfare.

Larry never went to college and instead started working for United Parcel Service. At age twenty-three, he moved to Florida to pursue his dream of being in radio. After a year or two in Miami, he convinced WAHR radio's general manager to let him hang around the station. Larry hardly ever left the station, learning how to rip newswire and watching the announcers work. Finally, in 1959, at age twenty-five, Larry got his first big break on air. He was told on a Friday that on the following Monday morning he would have his own show from 9:00 to 12:00 every morning and would do the news in the afternoon. For doing the morning show and afternoon news, WAHR would pay him a salary of fifty dollars a week.

Larry was so thrilled he was going to be on the air that he couldn't sleep all weekend. When he arrived at the station Monday morning, he was exhausted and scared to death. Ten minutes before 9:00, the general manager turned to Larry and asked, "So, Mr. Zeiger, what name do you want to use on air?"

Larry hadn't even thought about it and had no answer for him. Desperate, the general manager looked down at an open copy of *The Miami Herald* that happened to be flipped open to an ad for King's Wholesale Liquors. He asked, "Hey, how about Larry King?"

"Sounds fine to me," Larry answered, and Larry King was born. Larry then went into the studio to go on air for the first time. When he got his cue, he froze. His new show's opening music kept playing, and Larry turned the volume down to speak, but no words came out. He turned the music level back up, collected himself, and then flipped the level back down again. Still not a word. Larry envisioned his whole career ending before it even started. Suddenly, the general manager burst through the door and screamed, "Larry, this is a communications business, so communicate!"

And just as my mouth saved me on my first night of comedy, Larry's mouth saved him that morning. He cranked the music back down, parted his lips, and let the words pour out, "Hello, I'm Larry King. This is my first day and I've never done this before. I'm very nervous, but I'm going to talk to you and I hope you will listen."

Larry hasn't stopped talking since. One of the cardinal rules of broadcasting is, "If in doubt, leave it out." However, Larry has always been one to break this rule. If his gut instinct tells him to follow a line of questioning, even if he is unsure where it will take him, he will pursue it. Larry loves the whole world of broadcasting—being live, the happening of the moment, the sense of unrehearsed spontaneity, communicating with his guests and his audience. He doesn't use a different voice when he's on the air and doesn't pretend to be an intellectual. He just sees himself as an inordinately curious guy who's had the great fortune to get to learn about himself, other people, and the world by asking interesting people questions about their lives while millions are listening.

Two years after Larry's big debut, the owner of Pumpernik's approached him about doing a coffee-klatch radio show for WIOD in the deli. Larry loved the idea of working without any safety net in an off-the-wall, totally unrehearsed atmosphere and accepted the offer. Every day, different local people and celebrities, like Bobby Darin or Jimmy Hoffa, who happened to be in Miami, dropped in to chat on air live with Larry. This was a time before the advent of talk radio, so Larry's show in Pumpernik's was groundbreaking in that it was pure conversation, no music. Every broadcast was an exciting adventure because nobody knew exactly what was going to happen.

Soon Larry was doing a show called *Saturdays with Sinatra*, announcing sports on Sundays, and working as a columnist for *The Miami Herald*. By the late 1960s, Larry was known as Mr. Miami. Then in 1977, Larry moved to Washington, D.C., to do the first national all-night network-radio talk show. Initially carried by twenty-seven stations, this show was a nationwide forerunner of what we now know as talk radio. Shortly thereafter, he got his own D.C. TV show. When *USA Today* first appeared, Larry got his own weekly column, and then, in 1985, he was offered his own talk show every night from 9:00 to 10:00 on CNN. By the time Larry retired from radio in 1997, his show was carried by 485 stations.

Even though Larry has climbed to the top of the broadcasting world, he'll be the first to tell you that his life hasn't been without setbacks. He has lost his job twice, buried himself in debt, and filed for bankruptcy. Despite the personal and financial problems he's faced over the course of his life, he has never had an on-air problem, nor has any general manager he worked for ever frowned on anything on his shows.

I think the key to Larry's success is that he loves what he does. Larry sees broadcasting as a clean, wonderful way to make a living. He feels very fortunate to do what he always dreamed about doing and get paid for it. In fact, he'll tell you he hasn't worked a day in his life since he was twenty-one and delivering packages for UPS. This from a man who did a TV show, a newspaper column, and an all-night radio show every day of the week for decades.

The parallels between Larry's path to success and my own are rather striking: We started out broke, yet never felt poor. We reinvented ourselves. We rebounded from adversity. We gave ourselves permission to succeed, and realized that we could achieve success by doing what we loved to do. So, we followed our passions, played to our strengths, and stayed open to opportunity.

Later in this book, you will read of similar pathways culminating in successful business lives. Now that you have the "secret," however, perhaps you will be able to avoid some of the bumps we encountered on the way up the business mountain.

6

Perfection Can
Be Rehearsed

A big drinker was talking about how tough life had been for him. "Things were rough in the old days. There were times I had to live on nothing but food and water!"

O ne of my most exciting evenings as a performer was the night I opened for Dean Martin and Liberace at a benefit at the Fontainbleau Hotel in Miami Beach.

Dean Martin was an extraordinary man. I'll never forget the first time I met him. As I watched him perform on stage, I was struck by the attention he paid to every detail of his performance. While Dean always had the image of the big drinker, the swaggering, tipsy playboy, the truth is he was always a consummate professional. The glass of whiskey he held while he sang was usually tea. Dean was extremely serious and thorough about every aspect of his performance. He did long hours of rehearsals and sound checks. Every beat in his act, down to when he would sip his drink and slur his words, was practiced. He took every opportunity to better his presentation to the audience and never stopped trying to improve. In fact, the most important thing I learned from opening for Dean Martin was that successful professionals stay at the peaks of their fields not due to luck, but simply because they are more obsessed than anyone else with growing and perpetually improving what they do.

Martin wasn't the only one who was obsessed with being his best. Many of the comedians I saw had a real sense of how to work a crowd. Red Buttons, Milton Berle, Bobby Byron, Henny Youngman, Alan King, Buddy Hackett, Sammy Shore, Shecky Green—these were the masters at whose feet I sat night after night learning my craft. Nightclubs might sound like a strange place for a kid to grow up, but at that time I never saw any drugs, and the clubs were really pretty safe places for a teenager to hang out and to work on new jokes.

When I wasn't playing clubs, I loved to go to the movies. My favorite old-time movie palace was the Olympia Theater in downtown Miami. I went there just about every Saturday for seven years, from 1948 to 1955. For twenty-five cents, you could see a movie and a one-hour stage show featuring a ten-piece orchestra and five different acts. The star attraction would be a major name of the day, usually a singer but many times a comedian. I would sit in the fifteenth row until the movie was over, then I'd run up and grab a seat in the front row to watch the live performers. I loved to watch all the old pros because these comedians spent years and years honing their acts, so they knew exactly how to tell each joke and just how long to wait after the punch line. Vocal intonation, accents, timing —they had mastered it all.

As soon as they walked on stage, you knew you were watching polished professionals. They could connect with the audience immediately. Every little detail of the act that followed was fine-tuned for the appropriate audience reaction. They knew exactly how to dress, how to walk, how to make an entrance and an exit. For example, when their acts were introduced many of these vaudevillians would wait for three beats before walking onstage. In adapting this technique to my own entrances, I would always look behind me as I walked onstage, as if I was talking to someone, thus creating a certain mystique and theatricality. If you watch tapes of Johnny Carson on the old *Tonight Show*, you will see he did the same thing.

I think I learned more about how to walk into a meeting or work a roomful of people from great stage performers than from any classroom or other experience in my life.

Before you finish this book you may grow weary of reading the word "rehearse." But please understand that rehearsal is a proven method of making sure you are accounting for the informational and presentational details that characterize an effective sales, management, or other business performance. Don't be concerned that rehearsal or practice will lead to wooden presentations, because thorough knowledge of the details will permit you to tailor your approach to each customer or person you are addressing.

In commercial business, as in show business, it is not enough to simply continue to do well those things you have mastered; success is bred by a constant quest to improve every detail of your performance.

7

How to Survive
a Tough Audience

Two drunks are walking along Broadway in New York. One goes down into the subway by mistake. He comes up the other entrance and his friend is waiting for him.

The waiting drunk says, "Where were you?"

The other one says, "I was in some guy's basement. Has he got a set of trains!"

That joke always produced some good chuckles; but there was one hard night when it was greeted by stone silence. In comedy, as in the business world, I've had to face many tough crowds, and I've come to realize that standing on stage is really selling yourself.

Many times when I performed, people had purchased high-dollar tickets to see Connie Francis or Liberace, not to see me. I was just the guy they had to deal with until the real star came out. It was almost as if they were daring me to make them laugh. So I had to win them over to my side, or I was dead and so was my career. Ever since then, I knew that if I could leave an uninterested, impatient crowd feeling entertained, then I could win over anybody.

But exactly how did I manage to sway them to my side? Well, I saw myself as having a choice: I could panic, which would inevitably destroy my performance, or I could focus on relaxing and just doing my job as I'd done it so many nights before. Though I was nervous, I came out looking relaxed and always opened with my strongest material. As soon as the laughs started rolling in, I would get more comfortable and loosen up. Yet, no matter how well things were going, I knew I could never afford to totally relax, because a single misdelivered line could blow the whole thing.

Throughout my entire routine, I slowed down every time I started to speak too quickly, and stayed focused on the material and the audience. Fortunately, my efforts paid off in steady work up and down the East Coast, including engagements in the Catskill Mountains in upstate New York.

During the fifties, that area was still known as the Borscht Belt, the famed string of hotels and bungalow colonies popular among Jewish families looking for mountain air, kosher food, and entertainment as a summer retreat from New York City. For the thirteen weeks between Memorial Day and Labor Day, comedians, musicians, and singers could count on six or seven performances a week. For the most part, the million vacationers who summered in the Catskills were a relaxed, convivial group. It was an ideal place to try out new material and different ways to win over an audience.

Despite all of the fine tuning of my act, however, I encountered audiences that defied my efforts to win them over. One of the most difficult I ever faced was in a veterans hospital theater. But let me first give you a little history of this hospital.

During the booming 1920s, the ultraswank Biltmore Hotel was built in Coral Gables, Florida, by Coral Gables founder George Merrick and hotel magnate John Bowman. It opened in 1926 and was an immediate hit. Celebrity guests included the Roosevelts, the Vanderbilts, the Duke and Duchess of Windsor, Bing Crosby, and Babe Ruth. Gangster Al Capone even moved into one of the suites.

And no wonder. The Biltmore was resplendent with its landmark 315-foot central tower, beautifully appointed vaulted lobby, lavishly equipped theater, lush central courtyard, and massive swimming pool (still the largest hotel pool in the continental United States).

But the Biltmore's high times ended during the depression-ridden thirties. In the 1940s, the hotel was seized by the U.S. government and converted into a hospital for the Army Air Force and eventually the Veterans Administration. The once glorious sanctuary for the rich and famous became a linoleum-covered, antiseptic-smelling way station for injured soldiers.

The U.S. government realized that those troops needed entertainment as a diversion from their injuries. Since the hotel's theater remained intact, the Veterans Administration hired entertainers to perform at what had become a veterans' hospital. By the time I was performing in south Florida, the patients were veterans of the Korean War.

Some of the biggest names in show business played that veterans hospital theater. By this night in 1957, I had been hired to do my act numerous times and took a lot of pleasure in getting this audience laughing. God knows they needed it.

However, this one particular night turned out to be one of the biggest challenges of my whole show business career. My good friend, Mike Osman, and I had plans that night for a double date after my performance. We agreed that I'd pick him up on my way to the hospital, he'd watch my show, and then we'd go on our dates.

Mike and I walked past the hospital guardhouse and made our way to the theater. When we got there, the place was dark and deserted. We retreated to the information desk where the staff member found my name on the clearance list. He said my show wasn't going to be in the theater and that someone would escort us to where I was to perform.

A uniformed staff member appeared and led the way, pulling out a huge key ring like the jailer carries in Westerns. He opened a metal, prison-like door which he then locked behind us. He led us down a long, windowless hallway, opened a second metal door, and locked that one behind us as well.

I had been booked to perform my comedy act in the psychiatric ward. Heaven only knows what these men had been through in Korea for their minds to be so ravaged and unhinged. Clearly, I thought, a tuxedo-clad, fresh-faced comic was not going to penetrate the void they now lived in. But I had been hired to perform, and, as the saying goes, the show must go on. Mike stood in the back of the room, valiantly laughing and applauding as I did my thirty-minute act before 150 vacant-eyed patients who had no idea what was going on around them. No joke brought a laugh.

In a similar vein, there were nights at Leon & Eddie's when Rod Roberts had to perform before a mere handful of patrons, or just a single customer. In those situations, neither the lack of a real audience, nor Leon's non-payments, nor even the absence of response from the few or one who attended, compelled me to change my approach. Those occasions were useful at least as rehearsals, and I gave my best effort. Never give less in difficult circumstances, and you'll find you'll always be at your best.

Over the years since those performances, I've come to appreciate what a valuable lesson they taught me. Despite thorough preparation, I've occasionally walked into situations that were much worse than what I had anticipated. Each time, the temptation to cut my losses and escape was enormous. But I resolved to protect my reputation and salvage what I could. I've never suffered more than discomfort taking this approach, and I'm convinced that it has trained me for tackling the sort of highly uncomfortable situations every CEO has to face.

8

You Can't Juggle
Without Focusing

In the highly entertaining movie City Slickers, *a grizzled trail boss named Curly (played by the great Jack Palance) says to Mitch (a tenderfoot played by former stand-up comedian Billy Crystal) that he knows "the secret to life." When Mitch asks Curly what it is, Curly holds up one finger and tells Mitch that the secret is just "one thing."*

On one level, Curly was right. People who try to excel at too many things (even two, according to Curly), usually find their energies spread too thin to do exceptionally well at anything. On a different level, Curly was wrong. Life is so multidimensional, that to achieve happiness, people not only have to accomplish many things, but accomplish them simultaneously.

Since I started performing at age eleven, I learned intuitively that life in show business was a constant struggle. Performing while attending the University of Miami as a full-time student wasn't easy, but college education was important to my father and I didn't want to disappoint him. I would play the Miami clubs at night during the school year and do the Catskills or tour the East Coast clubs in the summer. It was a tough schedule, but I was young and my enthusiasm kept me going.

My ability to connect with an audience on stage helped me juggle my academic, personal, and professional lives. The only way to keep so many balls in the air, I learned, was to be extremely disciplined. When I was with friends or family, I had to focus exclusively on them and not think about new jokes for my act. When I was in the classroom or doing homework, I had to clear my mind of everything but the academic material.

In real life, there is much juggling to be done—family and home life, career, extracurricular activities like charitable work, exercise, and recreation. Everyone in business has to do it. Don't fight it. Manage it with focus so as not to neglect any of these parts of your life. Inevitably, there will be times when it seems your career demands are insatiable. But there always is time to communicate with your family, and to get in some exercise.

Actually, the juggling never stops; nor should you want it to stop. If it does, you will become a one-dimensional person with no life outside your work, and your career will suffer as a result because your ability to relate to people on a personal level will be diminished.

Curly might disagree, but maintaining all the enjoyable facets of your life are essential to your happiness; and focusing intently on whatever engages your attention at the moment is the key to successful juggling, and, as I'll discuss later on, one of the most important elements of business success.

9

Life and Career Crossroads

Hers had been a typical day. At work, she'd yelled at the receptionist, bawled out her secretary, verbally whipped a kid from the mailroom, thrown out four computer salesmen, threatened her beautician, cursed two drivers in front of her, fired the maid, warned her landlord because of a leak, and at eight-thirty at night, blushed when her boyfriend said, "Marry me and I'll be your protector!"

The most extraordinary of all the many accomplished and interesting people I met during those eleven years I worked in show business has to be a girl by the name of Phyllis Hollander. Her real name is Phyllis, but her family and close friends call her Phissy.

I met Phissy when she was fifteen and I was seventeen. She was pledging a high school sorority that was putting on a dance called "The Matzo Ball." The members had written a skit entitled *Time Matzos On*, which featured my band. Dances in those days, no matter who put them on, always had live music. There was no such thing as an "in person" disc jockey. DJs were only on the radio. The skit was a minstrel show; Phissy had to sing "Sweet Georgia Brown" and I would accompany her. The part called for her to intentionally sing it badly. It was obvious she didn't have to try very hard. She can still sing in a number of different keys—only all at the same time!

After that, we saw each other in school, working on various

plays. I was the stage manager and she was in the thespian society. We became friends from working on those projects together and through her sorority and my fraternity. By her senior year she started dating Barry Zimbler, who played the saxophone in my dance band. I was already attending the University of Miami, but quite often I would visit Miami Senior High School during the last period of the day, when the thespians had their class. Sylvia Furlong, the drama teacher, had been my favorite. She had always shown a sincere interest in me and my career.

During one of those visits, I had heard of Phissy and Barry's serious romance. I remember commenting to her, "Barry promised I could be best man at the wedding." It was after returning home from a three-month comedy tour of the Northeast and Midwest in 1958 that I discovered their romance was over. Neither of us was dating anyone at the time, and we became better friends. At an "open house" party her sorority threw, we danced to records and talked. When we had spoken earlier about going to this open house, I agreed to take her home. I later learned that this was a ploy on her part to avoid driving that night. I have officially proclaimed that to be our "first date." It was August 2, 1958.

We had a great time that evening, going for coffee and dessert with two other couples after the party. In those days, the cars we drove were all big enough to easily hold six people. All night the laughter never stopped. We discussed everything under the sun, including how to politely spit out watermelon seeds.

When I took Phissy home that night and gave her a brotherly kiss on the forehead, wishing her sweet dreams, I thought about how much fun we had together. In fact, to this day, Phissy still insists it wasn't her putting on any charm, but just our having a great time with the group. To me, though, it was all her, and I was falling in love.

As I started to fall for Phissy, I knew that I had to make some big life decisions. It would be immensely difficult to support a family as a comedian. I kept thinking back to something that Georgie

Jessel had told me backstage at the Fontainbleau two years earlier. Today, only a few may recognize Jessel's name, but in those days he was still a big star. He had headlined on Broadway in the original stage version of *The Jazz Singer*, before Al Jolson did the film version. Franklin Delano Roosevelt gave Jessel the unofficial title of "Toastmaster General of the U.S." Jessel was a beloved entertainer who had performed all over the world, married four times, and seen it all.

Picture this: I am seventeen years old, a fresh-faced innocent. I had just gotten off the stage at the Fontainbleau and was relaxing in the wings when Georgie Jessel grabs me and starts chatting with me about life. At first, I didn't know what to make of him, but then I started to realize he was a little tipsy and a little lonely. He had a good heart and he really wanted to give me some advice. He was an old man now who wore a crooked toupee and drank too much, but what he said to me has stayed with me for many decades as a great truth. Jessel looked deeply into my eyes and said, "Kid, if you ever fall in love and decide to get married before you make it to the big time, get out of the business—because it ain't gonna work!"

Sure, Jessel had been drinking that evening; yet, there was authentic wisdom in his words, and maybe some prophecy. Four years after my backstage encounter with Jessel, I had to decide between show business and Phissy Hollander. Do I marry her and get out of the business, or do I try to be the exception and stay with it?

I didn't really have to think about it for very long. I loved comedy, but I loved Phissy more, and I knew I didn't want to let her get away. So, as soon as I could save up a little dough, I bought her an engagement watch (didn't have enough money for a ring), and asked her to marry me. We were wed on November 29, 1959. We have been happily married ever since.

The financial insecurity of a career in entertainment, combined with my desire to marry Phissy, led me to say goodbye to the comedy stage. I was twenty-one and knew I had to get off the economic roller-coaster ride known as show business and find a more stable way to support me and my new wife. I had to get a "real" job, but to be honest, I didn't have a clue as to what I would do for the rest of my life.

I tried selling weekly newspaper cartoon-advertising packages to small businesses, but it didn't suit me. I even tried selling insurance for six months with Mutual of New York, but that didn't work out either. And in an incident I'll tell you more about later on, I asked my dad to get me a job driving a truck for the company he worked for, but he declined. My son Steven was born on September 22, 1960, and I wanted him to have the best of everything. But that would require money I didn't have.

You might understandably wonder why, in my case, selling cartoon ads and life insurance weren't "the answers," but selling pens was. Selling is selling, right? Wrong. To sell successfully, you have to believe in the product and its market potential. In these instances, I didn't.

The market for ads was too restrictive. It was comprised of very small businesses, and a sale to a particular type of business was exclusive. So, for example, if a plumber bought an ad, I was barred from selling ads to all other plumbers in the market area.

The market for life insurance wasn't limited, but selling policies ran into a personal idiosyncrasy: I just couldn't be upbeat talking about death as the condition for survivors receiving money. Yes, life insurance salespeople make good livings selling a valuable product which entails benefits well beyond payments to survivors, and I own substantial policies. Nevertheless, at that time in my life, because the policies' greater value couldn't overcome my emotional quirk, my heart just wasn't in selling insurance.

For eleven years, my passion had been show business. After exiting the stage, I knew that my "new vehicle" had to be something I could be equally passionate about. What was it?

Soon enough, I found my answer: selling pens. Pens greatly

appealed to me as useful, attractive and so diverse that their market potential is as unlimited as the imagination….and eventually they will run out of ink, thus providing the opportunity for another sale.

How should you go about finding your answer? I suggest you employ a disciplined method something like this: take early life inventory. Ask yourself what your proudest and lowest moments were. Analyze those achievements and bad times. Take out paper and a Pilot pen, or go to your computer, and write what you learned from those memorable experiences. Don't be modest; be honest. You will compose a catalog of your strengths and weaknesses, likes and dislikes. In short, you will gain an appreciation of what makes you tick, and see clearly the qualities upon which you should build your career and the mistakes you should strive to avoid repeating.

Once in a job, you should know within six months whether it's something about which you are passionate; and if you are, doing more than is required won't seem like work.

Must you do more than your assigned work to build a successful career in sales? I'll put it this way: the Broadway musical *How to Succeed in Business Without Really Trying* was fiction. Your assigned work should be considered the beginning. Here's a checklist of some of the things you should add:

❖ Constantly learn everything you can absorb about your industry: its jargon and customs, your products, your services, your existing and prospective customers, and your competitors and their products and services. Seek out the engineers and technicians who manufacture your products to learn how they're made, what makes them work, and what their capabilities are.

❖ If you do these things, the knowledge you gain will improve your sales techniques and negotiating skills. In addition to any training available to you as part of your job, studying relevant books and attending hands-on work-shops will further enhance these skills. Especially for sales techniques, rehearsal is an excellent way of attaining the confidence required for effective delivery. And, of course, the more presentations you make, the more accomplished and polished they become.

❖ Constantly look for ways your products and services may be improved. In this quest, listen to anyone who has a suggestion, particularly your customers.

❖ Constantly look for new ways consumers may use your products and services.

❖ Constantly search for new channels of distribution.

❖ Develop a proprietary attitude about your company; never say, "It's not in my job description."

If you make these practices your business way of life, you should eventually fall in love with selling and the business of business; you then are meant to succeed.

10

Career Choice by Irresistible Forces

A comedian tried to make his mark in personal appearances. The jobs became fewer and fewer. Eventually he joined a circus. His sole job was to follow the elephants and remove all signs of their having made a no-no. Another comedian saw him one day and said, "This is demeaning. Why don't you quit?"

The first comedian said, "And get out of show business?"

I had already done that, of course, but when I was twenty-two and between jobs, I was so broke that I regularly visited construction sites to find empty soda bottles to trade in for their two-cent deposit value. How's that for a contrast to performing on stage clad in a tuxedo?

I was tired of dead-end sales jobs. My car was getting run-down from all the miles I was putting on it, and to be honest, I felt as if I was getting run-down, too. But I had a family to support, and I was never a quitter, so I spent the next six weeks looking seriously for a job. I woke up every morning, put on a suit and tie, and made it my job to find gainful employment. Firmly believing that looking for a job *is* a full-time job, I pounded the pavement and pursued every lead I could.

Yet, the longer I remained jobless, the more I felt I was failing as a provider for my wife and son. In fact, Phissy's mother started to feel the same way and asked her daughter if she was starting to get worried about me.

"No, Mom," Phissy replied, "Ronnie wants too much out of life, and he knows that there's no one who can give it to him but himself."

Phissy still believed in me. In fact, she seemed to have more confidence in me than I had in myself. From the first time I met her, I had always come across with great self-confidence, but now my confidence was draining fast.

Just a few days later, Phissy saw a blind job ad for "The World's Largest Pen Company" in *The Miami Herald* classifieds. It turned out that the company that placed that ad was Bic, which actually was not so big then, but I appreciated the fact that they thought big. The ad required the applicant to send a letter to a box number at the newspaper. I applied and was granted an interview. When I showed up for the meeting, I was interviewed by Bill Clune, a Bic employee based in Philadelphia. He asked me how old I was. "Twenty-two," I replied. Bill closed his folder as he announced that the minimum age for the job was twenty-four.

Drawing on my sense of timing and remembering how as a ten-year-old I had "become" twelve to land my paperboy job, I reinvented myself again. Waiting half a beat, I shot back, "Okay, I'm twenty-four."

Once we agreed I was the required age, we hit it off really well, and I thought I had the job. My stomach dropped when he said that while he'd like to hire me, he needed to interview some other candidates and would call me. Thinking of my nonexistent finances and very existent wife and baby, I told Bill that I couldn't wait long. We agreed that he would call me in three days.

He didn't call. My desperation increased. My cousin Jack Sherwood had been asking me for weeks to come work with him at his insurance brokerage firm, but I had resisted. Despite my misgivings about selling insurance, I relented and called him. Instead of meeting at his office on Monday morning, he asked me to join him on an 8:00 a.m. call to an elderly client.

We knocked on her door at 7:55 a.m. sharp. She cracked the

door open a couple of inches, clearly not prepared for guests. She had forgotten the appointment. She asked if we could go to the nearby coffee shop and come back in forty-five minutes to give her time to dress.

Since Jack was buying, we sat at a booth and ordered breakfast. Just as I finished my scrambled eggs, Bill Clune walked over to my table. He had been sitting at the counter and saw us in the mirror that reflected all the booths.

Bill reintroduced himself as the guy who interviewed me at Bic. I am embarrassed to admit I was rude. Behaving as though my financial disaster was his fault, I nearly snarled when I said, "I thought you were going to call me."

"Sorry, but I've been really busy," he said. "But, can I talk with you for a moment now?"

"It's too late," I snapped, then motioned to Jack. "I'm working with Jack Sherwood now."

Bill didn't budge. He asked, "Well then, can I meet you at one o'clock?"

I dug in my heels and said, "No! I'm with Jack now, and we have things to do! If I meet with you, you have to give me the job. I can't mess around anymore. I have a family to support."

We agreed to meet at 1:00. By 1:05, I had the job.

I am a very pragmatic guy who doesn't usually speak in spiritual terms like "destiny" or "God's will," but in this case, who knows what cosmic forces were conspiring for my benefit and why? If Jack's client hadn't forgotten our appointment, we wouldn't have gone to the coffee shop. If Bill's home had been Miami, he wouldn't have stayed in a motel around the corner from the coffee shop. And if none of us had been hungry, I might be selling insurance today.

Sometimes we come to crossroads without even realizing it. To paraphrase Yogi Berra: I came to the fork in the road and took it, but it had to stab me in the leg first to get my complete attention!

* * *

When I got the job at Bic, I beat out sixty-five other applicants and received ninety dollars a week, which to me at that time was all the money in the world. My wife and I were thrilled, and I finally felt confident I would be able to support my new family.

Now let me give a little background on Bic Pen. What is now the Bic Pen Company was launched in the United States after the French company, Societe Bic S.A., acquired control of the Waterman Pen Company in 1958. Waterman was known as the inventor of the original fountain pen, in 1875. In 1960, following an extensive marketing test in Connecticut, the Bic ballpoint pen was introduced throughout the Northeast with tremendous success. In 1961, when I joined the company in Miami, sales and distribution coverage had been expanded to the Southeast.

Thus, I joined Bic just as it was poised for rapid expansion. While today the Bic brand has become a household name, it wasn't always so well known. In the early 1960s, the low-cost ballpoint pen market in North America was dominated by two brands—Scripto and Lindy.

Both Scripto and Lindy were selling an inexpensive pen in all distribution channels. Neither brand, however, did very much in the way of marketing. In this crowded field, Bic believed it could open new markets best through television advertising. First, a sales organization had to be hired. Bic told its salespeople to reach consumers wherever they shopped. Instead of using one blanket sales approach for all outlets, therefore, the company emphasized a variety of approaches. Because a consumer could purchase the same pen in a supermarket or a national variety store, the sales techniques used to persuade him or her to buy that pen in these different types of stores had to be very different.

As a result of this diverse sales philosophy, Bic chose not to hire salespeople with experience in selling pens. It is clear to me now that I was a good candidate to work for them. Ironically, once

I got hired, I assured my friends and family that this would only be a temporary thing. Little did I know that I would spend the rest of my life in that business.

In any case, please be encouraged by the fact that now, as in the past, experience in selling a specific product or service often is not necessary to get started in business as a salesperson. Even as a beginner you can achieve remarkably good earnings if you develop an affinity for selling. And you can do that if you believe in yourself and in the positive value of your products or services, and are determined to perfect your presentations. Developing such beliefs and determination is a big part of giving yourself permission to succeed.

11

Sink or Swim
Sales School

A salesman takes his wife along on a business trip to Las Vegas. On their first night in town, before going out to dinner, he finishes dressing before she does. He tells his wife that he's going to go wander around the casino and that he'll meet her there in twenty minutes.

So the salesman's in the casino hanging around the craps table when this beautiful hooker walks up to him and says, "Hey there, mister, you want to have a party?"

Curious to know the going rates, he answers, "Well, maybe. How much?"

She looks at him and says, "One hundred fifty dollars."

He laughs. "That's a little more than I wanted to spend."

"How much did you want to spend?"

"Five bucks," he says, trying to get rid of her.

She calls him every name under the sun and storms away.

A few minutes later, his wife finally comes down to the casino and as they're leaving the hotel to get a cab, he sees the same hooker standing by the front door. As he walks by her, she shakes her finger at him and says, "Uh-huh, see what you get for five bucks?" (Apologies to wives all over the world.)

N ow that I had a "real" job, I was determined to run with it. On my second day at Bic, I stumbled. I went to visit a small stationery store. I launched into an impassioned sales pitch to the owner. I did everything in the world I could possibly think of to get him to put up a display of Bic pens in his store. When it seemed as though I had finally convinced him, he looked at me and said, "Okay, what kind of terms do you people have?"

I didn't know what he was talking about. I'd never heard the word terms used in this context before. Quite frankly, I'd never even been trained. The day before, Bill Clune had just given me a bag of samples and told me to go out and sell, sell, sell. And now, I didn't know what to do. I did know that I wanted to close this deal, and I didn't want to appear stupid.

So I looked him right in the eye and said, "Terms? We get along with everyone."

He burst out laughing. "Kid, you wouldn't by any chance be new at this would you?"

I nodded and shrugged. This dealer was a nice man, and he felt sorry for me. So he gave me a little lesson.

"When I ask you," he said, "what kind of terms you have, I mean what kind of dating can you give me?"

"Oh, it really doesn't matter. Today's date, yesterday, tomorrow. Whatever you want."

He laughed again, and then he sat me down and taught me the meaning of dating and terms.

And the best part of it all was that he didn't cancel the order. I've always believed that if you want the order, you need to ask for it, and so, even though I was a novice salesperson, I didn't lose that order.

I'll admit I got lucky that time. As a salesman, like the one approached by the Las Vegas hooker, I should have known my dating and terms. But I can assure you of this: From then on, I realized that unlike Blanche DuBois, the faded Southern belle in *A Streetcar Named Desire*, my well-being could not "depend on the kindness of strangers." The embarrassment of ignorance I suffered that day propelled me to vow never again to be caught with my pens down. So becoming well prepared to make sales presentations became my Job Number One. Because there was no training program, I took it on myself to learn everything I could about Bic pens, and (obviously) industry sales terms. Drawing on my stage experience, I rehearsed my pitches. The result was that prospective customers believed I knew what I was talking about because I *did* know what I was talking about, and so delivered my presentations with persuasive conviction. No sales approach succeeds like one that is knowledgeable and confident.

Possessing those two qualities—knowledge and confidence —is crucial. The checklist on page 72 provides you with a pretty fair idea of the steps you need to take to develop and retain them. If mastering those steps seems intimidating, then remember this: seek to become an expert about the product or service you are selling, and practice your sales approaches. To reasonably expect even a small degree of success, you have to make at least that minimum effort.

12

To Stand Out, Stand Up

There was a priest I once knew by the name of Father Donnelly. His church urgently needed funds to renovate their old building. The church was in a poor part of town, however, and none of its members could afford to give any money.

So Father Donnelly turned to God. "Lord, please let me win the lottery this week, and I promise I will use all the money to renovate this house of yours."

But Father Donnelly did not win the lottery that week. So the next week, he turned to the Lord again, "Dear Lord, please, this week, let me win the lottery and I promise I will use the funds to glorify your name."

And again, Father Donnelly did not win. Now desperate, he decided to try one last time. "LORD, PLEASE! I promise you, if you let me win the lottery this week, we will turn your church into one of the most beautiful places in the whole world."

Suddenly, thunder crashed, lightning struck across the sky, and God appeared to Father Donnelly, saying, "Father Donnelly, I'd love to help, but please, meet me halfway. Buy a ticket!"

At my first sales meeting at Bic, I was an ambitious young (twenty-two, posing as twenty-four) salesman. The credit manager, Moe Maloney, found out I used to be a comedian, so at the end of our big sales conference, he urged me to get on stage.

Now, I wouldn't recommend this to anyone else, but after so

many years in show business I was very comfortable on stage, and I figured being in the spotlight might help jump-start my career. So, I grabbed the microphone. The company president, Bob Adler, was sitting right in front of me, and this was my big chance to make sure he knew who I was when our meeting was over that evening. There were a lot of new, young employees there, and I wanted to leave a lasting impression. So, I "bought a ticket"—took a chance — and started making jokes about him.

For example, though Bob is brilliant, he could be a bit caustic. I mentioned how his idea of a compliment is walking up to a young lady in the office and saying, "Oh, I see your face has cleared up!"

Everybody roared with laughter and I knew I was going to either lose my job right then and there, or be seen as a hot new up-and-comer.

Thankfully, Bob had a great sense of humor, and that night started me on a quick rise through the company. Bob sensed, I think, that if I had the confidence to stand in front of a large crowd and make jokes about everyone, including the head of the company, I had the confidence to sell Bic pens to anybody and everybody. And I did.

Having advanced to an assistant zone manager in Miami, I was soon winning sales contests and making a name for myself in the company. Shortly thereafter, I was promoted to Florida zone manager. Then, I was moved to Atlanta to be zone manager for a region that encompassed parts of seven states. It was while we were living in Atlanta that our daughter, Susie, was born, May 27, 1962.

We'd been in Atlanta only eleven months when Bic started opening new regions. I am a nester and hate moving, but I understood that relocating was necessary for success in the corporate world. When I was offered the plum zone of Chicago, even though it meant another move, I knew I had to seize this opportunity. Chicago was a great territory because it was so densely populated. Instead of having to drive across seven southeastern states, now I'd never have to leave Cook County, Illinois.

We lived in Chicago for three years, until I was promoted to sales manager of the new North Central region in Detroit, Michigan. After three and a half years in Detroit, I was named national sales manager, and we moved to New Haven, Connecticut. One month later, on March 28, 1969, our third child, Alan, was born.

Looking back, I believe the single greatest factor in my ascendancy at Bic was that I had a supportive wife who was always willing to endure one more geographic relocation and make one more personal sacrifice to help me on my way. But there were other major factors. I had a strong mentor in my immediate boss, Jack Paige, vice president of sales and marketing. Besides being a terrific boss, Jack was a bright, shining star in the Bic universe. His glow encompassed me and helped lift me through the ranks. I also made sure I remained visible in the company. I aggressively pursued every lead I was given, and I was always willing to pay my dues.

Much of this book deals with resilience in handling adversities in the forms of mistakes and just plain bad luck. But good luck, unmistakably, visits every life and business too. Be open to recognizing it, and willing to accept it. I had it at important points in my career from my second day with Bic when a good-hearted customer educated me about industry terms, to the times Jack Paige at Bic and later, Akira Tsuneto at Pilot, became my mentors. Although one cannot choose one's mentors, it is important to nurture those relationships should they occur. Don't allow false pride to turn you away from your good fortune by proclaiming you can succeed without help from anyone. While self-reliance is an admirable quality, it shouldn't be exercised in the extreme. Business, after all, is a collaborative effort, and you could do a helluva lot worse than have Lady Luck as your partner. Besides, good luck isn't all luck. You're more likely to attract helpful people, including would-be mentors, by projecting a positive image and attitude, and by taking timely risks *before* you see Father Donnelly's lightning bolt.

13

To Sell to the Head,
Speak to the Heart

An old friend was doing fund-raising and had been given a list of wealthy people and the charities, if any, they'd contributed to. He was encouraged to call those who were not currently supporting any specific cause. One of the people he called was particularly rude and grumpy on the phone. The records showed this grumpy man had done very little for charitable causes. When my friend pointed this out to him, the grump got very angry.

"Well," the grump shouted, "do your records also show I've got an old feeble mother? Do your records show I have a brother who is out of work and a sister with two kids who was abandoned by her husband? And if I don't help them, why should I help you?"

Some people are by nature generous while others are by nature stingy. Some are moved by their feelings while others appear to lack them. The older I get, the more convinced I am that we can't change others' natures. Whether working as a comedian, salesman, or CEO, however, I have tried to *understand* human nature. My livelihood has depended on developing deep insight into how people think, work, and behave. The better that understanding, the better my choices are and the more I can do to build our company.

I learned one of my most valuable lessons about human nature when I was at Bic. At that time, we were selling the Bic fine-point stick pen with a yellow barrel for twenty-nine cents. In an effort to stimulate sales, we started making it in white plastic in addition to the yellow. We used the same molds, added a little metal clip that probably cost one-tenth of a cent and charged forty-nine cents for what was the identical pen. And it sold like crazy!

A close friend liked the white pen better than the yellow one. It got to the point where she'd write only with the white one, not the yellow one anymore. She believed the white one was better. I tried to explain they were identical pens, but there was no use. What can you do?

Nothing, except sell more pens! I came to understand that people respond to the way a pen looks, feels, and writes as well as its point size, ink color, and type of ink. It's quite common for people to pick out a pen for logical reasons, then "fall in love" with it for purely emotional reasons. Let's face it, out of all of the everyday office supplies—paperclips, scissors, staplers—pens are personal. They are held in our hands for great lengths of time, placed in our pockets, carried in our purses and briefcases, laid on our desks, and placed within reach of our phones. Pens are presented as gifts, used with flourish in ceremonial signings, and some are even passed down from generation to generation. With pens we write love letters, make lists of baby names, and sketch plans for dream houses. Pens are fundamental tools for satisfying the human need to express ourselves personally and be understood. Once someone discovers a pen that feels good in the hand and writes smoothly, a sort of zealous loyalty is born.

Many people will write with only their favorite brand of pen. That's why in the large office supply stores, brand names dominate the pen aisle. Most of the tens of thousands of items in these stores—paper, folders, toner, tape—consumers view as commodities. Brand has little impact on purchasing decisions. But for pens, brand matters. Decisions to purchase are based on an interwoven matrix of logic and emotion. For that reason, in our marketing efforts we strive to appeal to the heart as well as the head. That's taking human nature into account.

To market and sell your products and services successfully, it is essential that you understand your products and services, your customers, and what drives your customers' decisions to buy your products and services.

14

"It'll Never Work"

An old friend once went to a big business conference in Miami Beach. He was staying at a lovely, small beach hotel. He knew he was going to be in seminars all day, so he decided to get in a little exercise before the conference started.

Arriving at the swimming pool bright and early, he was delighted to find it empty; he would have the pool all to himself. As he walked to the edge, he noticed a little old man sitting on a chaise lounge.

"How's the water?" he asked him.

"Luke varm," replied the man in a Jewish accent.

He shrugged, threw off his towel, and dove into the pool. The water was freezing! He screamed and jumped out. He ran shivering over to the old man and said, through chattering teeth, "You call that lukewarm?! That water's like ice!"

The old man shrugged his shoulders at him. "Mister, I didn't even go in, but to me, it luked varm."

It's important to be able to trust other people's opinions, but always be aware of who you're talking to and what their agendas are.

In 1972, it was my job to help introduce the Bic lighter to North America at the low price of $1.49. At that time, the number-one disposable lighter in the country was the Gillette Cricket. We were just a little pen company that had a share of the writing instrument market and no share of the disposable lighter industry.

In fact, this lighter was the first non-pen product Bic introduced. We viewed the lighter as a logical extension of our current product line since it was inexpensive, disposable, and of high quality. Moreover, it could be easily marketed through most of the trade channels we had already established for our writing instruments. It really differed from our pens only in that it had twenty-one rather than seven basic assembly parts and, as a flammable object, was subject to government standards.

I'm proud to say that within a few years of the introduction of what would become known as the Bic Butane, we put the Cricket out of business. How did we do it? Well, obviously, launching any new product is a highly complex and risky mix of procedures, and a multitude of factors influence that product's success. But I heartily believe that the launch was what got the Bic Butane into people's hands across the country. Once we did that, the lighter started to sell itself.

In planning our launch, Jack Paige and I decided that we could not afford to let others tell us if the waters "looked warm." We had a limited budget at a time when the general consensus in the industry was that you needed a huge budget to market a new item. We understood this line of reasoning, but believed we had to dive into the market and check it out for ourselves. Thus, we initiated a thirteen-cities-in-fifteen-nights promotional tour around the country. Everybody told us it was crazy. "Too many cities in too short a time," they said again and again. "It'll never work."

We believed otherwise. In every city, we set up invitation-only cocktail/dinner parties for our best Bic pen customers. I would warm up the crowd with a few jokes and a little shtick, then Jack would do a pitch for the Bic Butane. Customers were encouraged to bring their spouses. We invited the press and served everyone a fabulous meal. Sure, it cost the company a pretty penny, but it was still a lot cheaper than a big ad campaign—and it was a lot more personal. We received tremendous press and did lots of interviews. Instead of an impersonal national media campaign, we were right there face-to-face with our buyers. We didn't take any orders at the cocktail parties; it was soft sell. We just wanted to create awareness and good will. Later on, we had our salesmen pursue the leads. Let me tell you, it wasn't hard for them, because all of our customers were already sold on the Bic Butane.

The lesson here—and it is a significant one—is to avoid getting too comfortable with traditional approaches to business projects and problem-solving. "Tried and true" should not be equated with "can't miss." But whether you're a business neophyte or veteran, you can't prove that proposition unless you challenge the adequacy of conventional approaches and test the viability of innovative ones. Business progresses when unconventional solutions generating positive results flow from those challenges. Such progress takes different forms, most prominently introducing new ways to market existing products. When you read about Tom Stemberg, the Lender brothers, Irwin Helford, the Razor Point advertising campaign and the Dr. Grip marketing project, you'll see further what I mean concerning the importance of testing, and breaking, the rules.

Conventional wisdom in a given industry needs to be tested, for if every player always heeded consensus thinking, the industry would stagnate. The prize goes to those whose actions change conventional wisdom.

15

The Big Picture Includes Details

One afternoon when I had a few hours to kill before a performance in Miami, I went to the beach to get some sun. Pretty soon, a woman with a beautiful little boy set up an umbrella and spread out a blanket. She rubbed sunscreen on the boy, placed a hat on his head, and told him to stay within sight of Mommy. She stretched out on her blanket and watched her son run to the water's edge. Suddenly, a huge wave came out of nowhere and swept the child away.

The woman screamed in horror and ran into the water after him, but it was too late. The little boy was gone, carried beneath the waves. She sank to her knees, threw her head back, and pleaded to the heavens, "Please, God. He was my only child. My pride and joy. Bring him back to me and I'll be forever indebted to you. I'll go to church every Sunday. I'll do anything if I can just have my baby back."

And then, suddenly, lightning bolted, thunder boomed, and a gigantic wave crashed onto the shore, depositing the child, unharmed at her feet.

The woman picked up her boy, glanced down at him for a second, and then stared up at the heavens and said, "Um, excuse me, Lord ....HE HAD A HAT!"

O f course it's crucial to pay attention to the big picture, but in business, you also have to be insistent about the details. When I worked as a comedian, I learned from the masters, especially Dean Martin, to hone my act to perfection, or at least try to get as close to it as possible. After I left show business, I learned to apply that discipline offstage, too.

Let me give you an example. While at Bic Pen, I went into the office of my boss, Jack Paige. Jack played a major role in increasing Bic's sales volume from $1.3 million in 1960 to $120 million in 1976. Jack received many awards for his business acumen, including Outstanding Corporate Marketing Executive of the Year by the Gallagher Poll and New England Marketing Executive of the Year.

Jack had an open-door policy, and I had a great idea that I wanted to share with him. "Jackson (we used nicknames for each other), why don't we put out a red and green Bic pen Christmas-stocking-stuffer blister pack featuring a smiling Santa on the package?"

I was convinced this would sell big-time during the Christmas season. Now, you have to understand that at this time in the business, pens were all sold individually, so there was no precedent for a multipack of pens.

Jack looked at me, smiled, and said, "Sorry, Buddy Boy. It's not gonna fly. Forget it. What are the stores going to do with all the multipacks left over on December 26th?"

He was right. I left his office, disgruntled and depressed. But only a few hours later, he called me back in and said, "Ron, what if the Santa was perforated?"

"Excuse me?" I didn't know what he was talking about.

"Think about it, Buddy Boy. If we perforate the Santas on the multipack, then the day after Christmas, the dealers can just rip Santa off the card and they can continue to sell their stock of our multipacks instead of sending them back to us."

I smiled and looked at him. Of course, he was right. And, the perforated-Santa Christmas stocking stuffer multipack went on to become a huge seller. I had a good idea, but I still had not spent enough time thinking through the details. Fortunately, I was working with Jack, who had the vision to refine my idea and make it into a real winner. Jack's marketing brilliance was one of the biggest factors in Bic's meteoric success in America.

Another great example of paying attention to the details in the big picture comes from Bob Adler, former president of Bic Pen. Bob deserves tremendous credit for what he did with Bic in North America. Bob helped Bic emerge from the residue of a deficit-ridden company, and over a short period of time in the extremely competitive low-priced sector of the pen industry, he helped make Bic number one. Bob attributed his success to "numerous and good management decisions based on forty percent science and sixty percent intuition."

Bob's story is a great American success story. Following his graduation from the Wharton School of Business in 1955, he reported for his first day of work as a junior accountant at the old Waterman Pen Company. The day before, the Naugatuck River had flooded the plant and when Bob showed up, instead of being shown to his desk, he was handed a shovel and told to help clean out the mud that had collected on the floor of the plant. Believe me, he didn't say shoveling mud was not in his job description, and nine years later at the age of thirty-one, Bob Adler was named president of Bic.

He immersed himself in every aspect of the company and became conversant with every detail. He regularly walked around the plant, always remaining visible and accessible to the employees. He referred to statistics, but always valued human instinct above numbers.

In terms of leadership, Bob stressed to me that a leader gets paid to make decisions. In many instances, there is really only one way to go. In these cases, making the decision is the easy part. The hard part happens after the decision is made. What's important then is that a leader be present to insure that the decision turns out right. The decision is not as important as the outcome. Many people fail to understand this concept. At Bic, Bob had a clear vision of the big picture, yet kept a sharp eye on the details of the actions required to have that vision realized.

Along these lines, there's an analog in the political arena involving Senator Bob Graham of Florida. Bob and I attended Miami High School together from 1953 to 1955; while I was active in the drama department, he was president of the student council, a harbinger of what would become a great political career. As part of his campaigns for governor and senator, he would go to different locations in the state, and take all sorts of jobs for a day at a time in attempts to experience a little of what "regular" people encountered in their lives, and to converse with them about their concerns. Bob gained invaluable knowledge about what mattered to people, and the voters so admired his efforts at staying in touch, he was elected governor and to three terms in the senate.

Perpetually paying attention to details is one important quality that distinguishes a successful businessperson from an ordinary one. It is a practice you should follow in your every effort, from the time you are just deciding on a career to the time you retire. I've afforded you suggestions about a disciplined approach to use in determining whether a business career will suit you, and if you begin in sales, how to employ details in fashioning and improving sales techniques, including attending to the details of your personal appearance. Take this emphasis on details to heart and it will help you develop the kind of self-confidence that will inspire anyone with whom you are dealing to have confidence in you.

Once you are elevated to the Board Room, remember that an executive cannot succeed or make decisions beneficial to the company by isolating him- or herself in an office, content with devising or evaluating big picture policy. He or she must become and stay aware of the details of the business. This is not the same as micro-managing, which involves distractions to be avoided; but, rather, is maintaining close contact with the products and people that make the company function.

Where does one get the time to do these things? By mastering the art of juggling (discussed earlier), by careful scheduling, and by delegation of responsibility to cover any obligations you cannot discharge while attending to the details. (Personally, being something of a "control person," I'm much more accomplished at scheduling than delegating, but thankfully, this deficiency has not caused great problems—just a little lack of sleep.)

In executive performance, you would do well to follow the examples of Jack Paige, Bob Adler, and Bob Graham, but however you do it, make certain you stay in touch with the details that should inform your business decisions. After all, it's those decisions and follow-up actions that help *create* the big picture—the company's mission.

16

The Power of Goals

A guy who was crazy about golf was having trouble with his game and went all over the city looking for a course that suited him. One day, he showed up at a brand new public course. There was a big line to get on the course, and he was in a rush. So, he introduced himself to a group of three Baptist ministers who needed a fourth. The ministers were happy to include him, and onto the course they went.

Three hours later, this guy was shocked and amazed. The three ministers had shot 69, 70, and 71, while he had shot 109. He had to ask, "Excuse me, but what's your secret?"

One of the ministers walked over to him and said, "We are very religious men, son, and since we lead such pure and simple lives, God rewards us with great golf games."

The golf fiend took what the minister said to heart and joined the church. He got baptized and went religiously, obeying all the precepts and praying fervently.

A year later, he bumped into the three ministers again at the same course. They agreed to shoot another round of eighteen with him.

Three hours later, the results were the same as the year before. The ministers shot 69, 70, and 71, while the golf fiend shot another 109.

He was exasperated and said to one of the ministers, "I don't understand it. I got baptized and went to church religiously, and still I've gotten no better."

The minister looked at him and said, "May I ask, son, what church did you get baptized in?"

"Trinity Baptist Church."

All the ministers nodded and laughed. Then, one of them put his arm around the golf fiend and said, "Sorry to tell you this, son, but Trinity Baptist is for tennis."

I t's important to define goals for yourself as well as for the people in your company. If you don't, you might end up with a lot of people working very hard and still achieving very little. Avoid this type of frustrating situation by always making sure that the organization's goals are clearly delineated to all.

In the early 1960s, the Bic Pen Corporation was an unknown French firm trying to sell an unknown brand of pens in North America. By 1974, Bic had almost 70 percent of the U.S. market, distributing more than 2 million writing instruments per day through more than 200,000 retailers. When I was assistant zone manager in 1961, Bic was selling 8 million units a year. By 1974, Bic was selling 2.5 million units a day. Everyone had said that:

A. Bic couldn't sell 5,000 feet of writing in one unit and succeed ("5,000 feet of writing in one unit" means that one pen contains enough ink to write a line that is 5,000 feet long).

B. Bic couldn't have the biggest sales force in the writing instrument industry and make money.

C. Bic couldn't advertise a nineteen-cent pen on TV and turn a profit.

The naysayers were wrong. Bic achieved all of those goals and was on top. There were many reasons for its success, including the leadership of President Bob Adler, VP of Marketing Jack Paige, and Treasurer Alex Alexiades. I'd like to think I also had a hand in Bic's success. I believe that one thing I did well during my Bic years was clearly articulating and emphasizing the branding of Bic pens through the power of personal selling efforts, backed up by sales promotion activities. Our sales force was the largest in the industry. As I mentioned earlier, when Bic initially developed its sales force, management avoided hiring people with experience in pen sales because they did not want salespeople to start out with pre-conceived ideas about how to sell pens. Rather than allowing each salesperson in a territory to call on all types of customers, Bic's sales force was organized so that each salesperson specialized in selling to only certain types of institutions in a specific marketing channel. For example, in the New York metropolitan area, Bic had one or more salesmen who specialized in selling to only one of the following types of customers:

❖ Wholesalers for independent retail drug and sundry outlets
❖ Drug and variety chain stores
❖ Food wholesalers and retailers
❖ Commercial users and office suppliers
❖ Premium and specialty advertising suppliers

Although this degree of specialization was unorthodox for selling a one-product line, we believed our specialized selling efforts were a major element in achieving our large market share. To augment our personal selling efforts, Jack Paige also instituted the use of premiums as a sales promotion method to entice both trade and commercial buyers to purchase in large quantities. Each of these tactics was part of the company's overall strategy to achieve specific goals.

When I joined Pilot, I used a goal-setting management style derived largely from the writings of Napoleon Hill to lift sales above the $1.2 million plateau. It's still effective and today reaches beyond the sales and marketing teams to each of our employees.

One thing we stress, particularly in sales, is that easily attainable goals, even if improvements, are goals set too low. We realize better results from the extraordinary efforts our people take to accomplish goals just beyond reach. In fact, sometimes, they exceed all expectations and achieve the unachievable.

In addition to setting goals, you need to create plans of action. They will help you achieve your goals without missing steps or jeopardizing the company. One plan I hope you'll never need is a crisis management plan. When a crisis hits, as it may, turning to a prepared plan will insure that you know what to do, how to do it, and when to do it—knowledge especially valuable when you're under attack. We are judged not by how we handle simple and easy situations, but how we manage under fire. Setting goals and establishing plans for the best is good leadership; preparing for the worst is smart leadership. It also helps to be in the right place. Before much more time went by, I would discover that for further advancement, Bic had been my Trinity Baptist.

17

Starting Over

A group of businessmen go to Alaska to hunt moose. When they get to Juneau, they hire a young pilot with a Piper Cub to take them to the tundra where all the moose hang out. The pilot flies them a hundred miles into the tundra, and as soon as the businessmen get out, they see a huge moose standing right in front of them.

They take out their guns, and Bam! Bam! Bam! they bag their moose. The hunters are overjoyed, but the pilot is not happy. He tells them that his little plane won't be able to make it back with such a large, heavy moose. He suggests they just cut off the antlers and bring them back as souvenirs. But the businessmen want the whole moose. The pilot argues with them some more, but the hunters insist and slip the pilot an extra hundred bucks.

So they pack the moose into the little plane, and miracle of miracles, they are able to take off. Forty miles from Juneau, however, the plane gives out and nose-dives. The pilot executes a crash landing without anyone getting a scratch. They all get out of the plane, but only the pilot is scared and distraught. He looks up and sees the businessmen hugging and dancing with each other. "Guys, why are you so happy?" the pilot asks. "It'll take us days to reach civilization now."

And one of the businessmen answers, "Yeah, but we crashed twenty miles closer to Juneau this year than we did last year!"

When you're faced with a challenge, you should embrace it; but also understand that each challenge comes with the possibility of failure. When failure happens, as it will, never allow it to get the best of you. Accept it, figure out why you failed, and make sure it doesn't happen again.

The right attitude toward success and failure will ensure your persistent efforts pay off. After many years of working very hard at Bic and earning five promotions, for example, I was suddenly and inexplicably let go. Well, I soon discovered that my firing wasn't exactly inexplicable. There are a lot of factors involved in the running of a large company. In my case, the chairman, Marcel Bich, wanted to appoint his son national sales manager to be in position to take over the company. Since that was my job, I had to be terminated.

So there I was, driving home Friday afternoon, January 3, 1975, not knowing what I was going to do. My daughter, Susie, was having a slumber party with a bunch of other girls at our house that night, and I had promised to take my older son, Steve, to a hockey game. I couldn't imagine how I would face, or what I would say, to either of them—not to mention Phissy.

When I got home, I kept my mouth shut, sat at the dinner table with the family, wished the slumber party girls well, and went to the hockey game with Steve. When I returned home, I said goodnight to the kids and joined my wife in bed. I couldn't hold out any longer. Finally, I blurted out, "Bic fired me. I don't have a job. They gave me seven months' severance and when that runs out, I don't know how I am going to make the mortgage payments or what we are going to do."

Phissy was upset, but more for the anguish I was feeling than over me being out of a job. Her confidence in me gave her a very different point of view. She saw opportunity where I could only see despair.

"This is the chance you've waited your whole life for," she told me. "You've got seven paid months to fulfill your dream of finally having your own business. Think about it. Without a boss breathing down your neck, you are finally free to take risks."

She was right. For years, I had dreamt of running my own

business. I always felt deep down that if I had come from a more affluent background or didn't have family obligations, I would have started my own company. Sure, when you're in your own business, there are no guarantees that you'll make it, but if things go bad, you know you'll be the last person to walk out the door. A person running his or her own business is in charge of his or her own destiny.

The more I thought about it, the more my sadness lifted. My wife was right. I had just been too wrapped up in my own ego and the shock of being fired for the first time to see for myself the vast opportunity that was now open to me.

I tried to envision opening my own company, but I felt the responsibilities of a mortgage, three children, and orthodontist payments precluded such a risk. I knew I needed to find a new job.

Though I'd been fired from Bic, the Fates weren't quite done weaving pens into my professional life. Just as some cosmic force propelled me to Bic in 1961, I was nudged back toward the world of writing instruments. And I was just as stubborn in resisting destiny's nudges in 1975 as I had been in refusing Bill Clune's request for a meeting in that Miami coffee shop fourteen years earlier.

In the late sixties and early seventies, Pilot pens were sold in the United States by a franchised agent, a company in the South Bronx named Elta Industries. By 1972, their sales rose to $1 million a year, then hit a plateau.

In 1969, four months after Phissy, the kids, and I moved to Connecticut so I could take my fifth promotion at Bic, I met Bob Grodd. Bob was a roofer and owned Premiere Roofing Company with his brother. They eventually built that business into one of the biggest roofing companies east of the Mississippi. At any rate, Bob became one of my closest friends.

About a year before Bic let me go, Bob and his wife went to a resort in Puerto Rico for a respite from the cold. While sitting by the pool, they met Harold Rosenberg, a fellow vacationer. Harold was one of three partners who owned Elta Industries. The Grodds and Rosenbergs exchanged the usual where-are-you-from, what-do-you-do niceties. When Bob discovered Harold was from New York and in the pen business, he naturally asked, "Do you know Ron Shaw at Bic?" Harold said that we had met (although I have no recollection of meeting him). They exchanged business cards. Once home, Bob put Harold's card in his desk and forgot about it.

Despite Phissy's belief that my being fired was an opportunity instead of a tragedy, I still felt wretched. I called Bob that first weekend and told him the bad news. Bob showed up at our door to lend his support and throw in his indignant "How could they! They're fools!" and a couple of other phrases best not to print. He also said that when he was in Puerto Rico the previous year he met a guy in the pen business. He volunteered to give him a call if I wanted. I may have just had the wind knocked out of me, but I found my show business chutzpa quickly enough. While moving up at Bic, I had met a lot of people in top positions at strong companies, I told Bob. I was pretty certain that with a few phone calls and interviews I'd land on my feet. I told Bob, thanks but no thanks. I'd be fine.

Soon after Bic let me go, a small story appeared in *The Wall Street Journal* and the business section of *The New York Times*. Bic was publicly held then, and certain activities had to be reported. The company had distributed a news release announcing my departure and diplomatically reporting that I was "pursuing other interests." That same day, I received a phone call from Mr. Ryouhei Yamada, the president of Pilot Corporation of America, makers of fountain and other pens. He said Pilot wanted to reclaim the rights to sell their pens directly in the United States, doing away with the franchise arrangement. He asked if we could meet. I had interviews lined up with a few large companies and didn't want to waste time with some obscure pen outfit. I politely told Mr. Yamada that I wasn't interested.

A couple of weeks and several interviews later, Mr. Yamada

called again. Pilot needed a sales and marketing director, and he asked if we could meet. I had new interviews scheduled with major corporations and was confident I'd find a big job with one of them. For the second time, I told Mr. Yamada that I wasn't interested.

By the end of February, I had no written job offers from any of the large companies I liked. Though I had five months of severance remaining, I was getting anxious. Plus, I like to work and was restless. Bob came over for a social visit and said he had found that pen guy's business card, then handed it to me. I noted that Harold Rosenberg's company represented Pilot pens and told Bob about Mr. Yamada's phone calls. Bob convinced me to let him call Harold.

By the time of Bob's call, Elta Industries and Pilot Corporation had reached an agreement that would return all rights to sell Pilot pens in the United States to Pilot Corporation of America. According to the terms, Elta's three partners would do very well as long as Pilot did well. Harold now had greater incentive to make Pilot sales break that $1 million plateau. After Bob talked with Harold, Harold called Mr. Yamada to tell him about this great pen salesman who was available. Mr. Yamada told Harold that he had already called me twice and couldn't get a meeting. Harold called me and pressed me to at least meet him and Mr. Yamada in Manhattan for lunch. Since I had no job offers and my prospects were narrowing, I agreed. They launched a hard sell during our meal. I agreed to a second meeting at Pilot's facility in Long Island City in Queens.

A stage set designer creating a dingy work environment could have used this place as the model. Pilot's entire operation in America occupied a windowless five-thousand-square-foot former taxi garage. The neighborhood was grimy, the building was gloomy, and it was a two-and-a-half hour trip from our house in Connecticut. However, I knew the pen business and became intrigued by the challenge of taking this little-known company stuck at $1 million in sales and building it into something much larger. I wouldn't have Jack Paige or anyone else to mentor me; I'd have to go the distance on my own. I wasn't thrilled about the commute and didn't want to move again, but Mr. Yamada agreed that if I could lift sales up to $10 million, Pilot would move to Connecticut.

Fourteen months after Bob Grodd sat beside a pool in Puerto Rico and exchanged business cards with a stranger, I was back in the pen business—easily "twenty miles closer to Juneau."

While between jobs, I hadn't, but I should have, applied an important lesson I learned performing comedy. I loved telling jokes and getting big laughs. However, there were nights when I didn't connect well with the audience and the big laughs never came. On those nights, it seemed I didn't have what it takes to make it in comedy. In a way, I think having my very first night as a comedian go so well was a mixed blessing. Getting all those laughs at the military base that night sucked me into the limelight, but from then on, I compared every performance to the perfection of that first time. And in the end, how could any other night compare?

On those nights that I bombed as a comic, I'd go home and feel sorry for myself. But when I woke up the next morning, I'd force myself to think about all the little victories I had achieved the night before, the jokes that *had* worked, the new things I did that were getting laughs, and I'd start to feel a whole lot better.

Despite Phissy's encouragement, I didn't focus on the positive aspects of my situation after being terminated at Bic. If I had, I'm convinced my anxiety would have been lessened. Should you find yourself similarly situated, concentrate on the positive possibilities, for even though you ultimately may not pursue the ideas that lift you up, the important thing is that you are uplifted. Your thought processes and creative juices then will be rejuvenated, and facilitate getting resituated.

18

Taking Risks in Advertising

Sitting on the side of the highway waiting to catch speeding drivers, a state highway patrol officer sees a car puttering along at twenty-two miles an hour. He thinks to himself, "This driver is just as dangerous as a speeder!" He turns on his flashing lights and pulls the driver over.

Approaching the car, he notices there are five old ladies inside—two in the front seat, and three in the back—all wide-eyed and white as ghosts. The driver, obviously confused, says to him, "Officer, I don't understand. I was going exactly the speed limit! What seems to be the problem?"

"Ma'am," the officer replies, "you weren't speeding, but you should know that driving slower than the speed limit can also be a danger to other drivers."

"Slower than the speed limit? No, Sir, I was doing the speed limit exactly—twenty-two miles an hour!" she says proudly as she points to a sign beside the road.

The highway patrol officer, trying to contain a chuckle, explains to her that "22" was the route number, not the speed limit.

A bit embarrassed, the woman grins and thanks the officer for pointing out her error.

"But before I let you go, Ma'am, I have to ask—is everyone in this car okay? Those women in the back seat seem awfully shaken, and they haven't uttered a peep the whole time."

"Oh, they'll be all right in a minute, Officer," she answers. "We just got off Route 116."

I t's easy to get caught up in your own mindset, to rely too heavily on the "we're right, they're wrong" mentality. You must always be aware that just because people don't interpret things the way you do, their alternative ideas are still worth considering. Hell, you might be wrong. And once you give credence to other notions, those new concepts just might help you speed past the competition.

During my business life I've seen this phenomenon many times. When I first joined Pilot Pen, for example, I wanted to run a national advertising campaign. I say "national" in that I wanted to put a few small ads here and there in national magazines. Keep in mind, Pilot had hit a $1 million sales plateau in the United States, and we had no advertising budget. So I went to Japan to ask the chairman of the board to free up $75,000 to buy ads in regional editions of magazines like *Time* and *Newsweek* for our ad campaign.

Picture this: I'm in the chairman's office in Tokyo making my pitch. The head of the company is nodding and smiling at everything I say; he can't look more pleased with my presentation. Having never been to Japan, I assume I'm doing great and will definitely close the deal.

Then, at the end of the presentation, the chairman stands up, expresses profuse admiration for my intentions, and says, "Shaw-San, this is a wonderful plan. Now, go back to America and sell enough pens so that you have enough profits to afford to do this advertising!"

Needless to say, I was very disappointed. I returned to the United States, borrowed the $75,000 we needed, and launched the company's first ad campaign. Borrowing money from a bank for an ad campaign is very risky, and I generally wouldn't recommend it. However, I believed in the campaign so deeply that I went forward. I always advise businesspeople that, if they so firmly believe in the concept or product they're pushing that they would spend their own money on marketing it, then, in these extreme cases, they should just go for it.

And so we did. But what was it that made me a true believer in Pilot pens? That first "national" ad campaign I so desperately wanted would sell Pilot's Razor Point pen. When I first joined the company, the Razor Point was our second-best seller, but that wasn't really saying much since overall sales were so low. Our problem was that the average consumer saw the Razor Point as a niche pen used only by architects and other design specialists, a technical writing instrument. I saw the Razor Point as a truly unique product that should be enjoyed by a wide array of consumers, and so we started to market it across the board.

Now, to be honest, at this point Pilot was struggling to gain a foothold in North America. The company was an industry leader in Japan, but its American division was near bankruptcy. We were a small company that hardly anybody knew about in the American pen market, and my mandate was to grab as much market share as possible. I spent much of my time and energy in those first years with Pilot on advertising, public relations, and marketing. After a concerted promotional push, we were able to make the Razor Point a huge seller that appealed to consumers engaged in all different professions. We convinced the public that anyone can write with an extra fine point pen. And within a year or two, the massive sales of Razor Point proved to be the key factor that saved Pilot from extinction in North America.

Sure, it was a risky proposition to try to market a so-called specialty product beyond its known market. In the end, though, my intuition proved correct. There really was a market beyond engineers for the Razor Point, but that market had to be educated. That's what our marketing campaign did, and that's how the Razor Point and Pilot gained a good share of the American pen business. Sometimes the key to making your company a success is already in the company.

Expansion of the Razor Point market is a good example of my earlier suggestion that to enhance your sales and marketing ability, you should take constant inventory of potential new applications and types of customers for your products. Especially in the case of an established product with good sales, it is easy to relax into a trap of complacency. My message to you here is to build on the solid foundation a successful product provides by thinking creatively. (There, I've made good on a promise to myself to avoid saying "think outside the box.")

When I started at Pilot, I had many years experience selling pens and over a decade of experience in show business. So when we created that first advertising campaign, I opted to use humor. At that time, many companies shied away from humor in their advertising, but I knew how powerful it was when done properly. We had this niche pen, the Razor Point, and humor might just be the key to make it known and accepted by all consumers.

I knew if we could use humor, not comedy, we could sell a lot of pens. That is, rather than go for the big laugh that would obscure the product, we promoted our pens by making the reader or viewer smile and think. From day one, my goal with advertising has always been to create consumer recall and retention, and I knew that the key to both was making the consumer feel good.

We entered the print advertising arena with something a bit unconventional. We bought a full-page ad, with half of the page devoted to the headline, "Is it sick to love a pen?" The other half showed a woman lying on a couch in a psychiatrist's office, telling the doctor seated behind her that she fears she's gone out of her mind over love for her pen. Her doctor assures her that there is nothing abnormal with her as long as the pen she has fallen in love with is a Pilot.

Using humor as we did in this campaign is always risky, because people respond to it in different ways. But we believed the benefits would far outweigh any potential downside. And the results proved our instincts correct. This campaign, developed by ad executives Don Aaronson and Stan Pearlman, owners of AMS

Advertising, was wildly successful. The comedic take we employed really helped Pilot get good product attention and retention.

It wasn't a campaign intended to produce belly laughs, nor did it, but it was cute, and it allowed us to take a little-known product, the Razor Point, and turn it into a bestseller. In addition, it helped us take a relatively unknown company in America—Pilot—and turn it into a recognized brand name.

We've all heard the clichés: "no risk, no reward," "no guts, no glory," and the like. There's truth in most clichés, and there certainly is truth in these two. In making business decisions, of course, you need to be able to differentiate risky actions from reckless ones. How do you accomplish that feat? Here's one way: First, relying on your (or a trusted person's) experience, you estimate the tangible and intangible costs and results likely to be produced by established methods. If those results seem inadequate, bring to bear all the creative thinking you can muster to devise new practices, and estimate their costs and results. You now have a comparative risk-reward or cost-benefit analysis. Assuming you are able to project better results from putting your innovative ideas in effect, how do you know whether they will succeed? The only answer to that question is that you can't know. No one can. That's why they call it "risk." But you can and should know what your instincts are telling you about these inventive ideas; and if they are sending you predominantly positive vibrations, it's time to step out and seek the reward that justifies the risk.

When you're driving on the highway, it's important to pay attention to the speed limit. In business and life, however, it's often necessary to break the rules and take risks to move forward.

19

Publicize Your Name

A long time ago, the king of Spain had a personal servant who had the annoying habit of exclaiming, "This is wonderful!" after every event.

One day, the king was on a hunting expedition in Africa. His servant was loading and preparing the guns for him. At one point, the servant handed the king a gun that he must have loaded wrong, because when the king fired it, it backfired and blew his thumb off.

The servant observed the situation and, as was his habit, declared, "This is wonderful!"

The king was furious. "No! This is NOT good!" he yelled at his servant and immediately had him locked up in jail for his transgression.

Six months later, the king was on another hunting expedition in Africa when he was ambushed and captured by a group of cannibals. They dragged him off to their village and proceeded to tie him up and prepare a fire and boiling pot. As they were lifting him into the pot, they noticed that he was missing a thumb. In their culture, it was forbidden to eat anyone who was less than whole because they believed it would bring extreme bad luck to the tribe, so they quickly untied the king and set him free.

On his return to Spain, the king ordered the release of his old servant. When the servant returned to the castle, the king apologized to him and explained what had happened.

"So you were right," he said. "It was wonderful that my thumb was blown off, and I'm sorry for sending you to jail for so long. I feel badly for doing that."

"No," the servant replied. "This is wonderful!"

"What do you mean, 'this is wonderful'?" asked the king. "How can it be wonderful to sit in jail for six months?"

"Because if I had not been in jail," replied the servant, "I would have been with you."

The success or failure of a company lies in the ways management deals with the bad and good unforeseen occurrences of everyday business. For example, when we heard about the upcoming signing of the peace treaty between Israel and the PLO in 1993, we were intensely curious to learn if Yitzhak Rabin or Yasser Arafat would use a Pilot pen. However, when asked by a reporter about the pen that would be used, Rabin replied that as a representative of the common people, he did not want to use a fancy pen, but instead whatever ordinary plastic pen was in his pocket at the time. So, we realized all we could do was wait and see if he would go with Papermate, Bic, or Pilot.

And wouldn't you know it? At the moment of the signing, Rabin pulled a blue Pilot V5 out of his pocket and used it to sign the accord.

I witnessed this event on CNN and was ecstatic. I immediately called our head marketing guy and asked him what he thought we could do with this news. He answered blandly, "Well, we should probably get a copy of the videotape and enter it into our archives."

Wrong answer! This was not just an archival moment; it was a great marketing opportunity, and I decided to handle it personally. I got on the phone with our advertising agency and we generated an immediate full-page newspaper ad campaign with a close-up photo of our pen being used to sign the accord. My son, Steve, wrote the headline: "There's a line between war and peace. This one was written with a Pilot pen." We believed this ad merited going into every paper in the country, but happily settled for the top twenty-five markets and thereby avoided busting our advertising budget.

For many people, this would have been the end of the peace pen, but as soon as the ad campaign was placed in the papers, we had another brainstorm. Maybe we could get our peace pen ad story picked up as a news item. I called our gung-ho public relations firm, PR News, headed by Jim Plunkett, and he pitched the story to a contact at the Associated Press.

Before we knew it, besides the twenty-five papers, we also had a news story about our peace-pen ad campaign in almost every paper in the world. What a coup! We were able to take a half-million-dollar ad campaign and get $20 million worth of positive publicity out of it. Now that's what I call taking advantage of an opportunity and capitalizing on it. Clearly, a company's success depends on how it creatively deals with unforeseen circumstances.

This brings me to a story about a special CEO. Thousands of years ago, Moses had a PR guy who followed him everywhere he went. The guy's name was Sam. Moses paid Sam a good deal of money to make sure he was highly publicized throughout the land, and to ensure that everyone knew where to find him.

When Moses and the Israelites got to the Red Sea, Moses asked Sam, "Where are the boats?"

"I'm sorry, Moses," Sam said, "I was so busy with all the press releases, I forgot to order the boats. Boat ordering isn't exactly in my job description anyway."

Moses was extremely angry. "Sam! You've really messed up here. What do you expect me to do now? Raise my staff and ask God to part the Red Sea?"

"Hey, boss," Sam said, "if you can do that, I bet I could get you two pages in the Old Testament!"

Retail sales obviously are heavily dependent on word getting out to the consuming public, and advertising, public relations and word-of-mouth are the ways the word is spread. Advertising usually is handled by paid professionals (with management oversight). Public relations (seen by some as "unpaid" advertising) also frequently is an outside function. However, I consider it to be a hands-on management responsibility as well, because in-house executives with media contacts may be able to recognize and respond more quickly to positive events affecting the company.

Public relations is a huge part of business these days. I don't know a CEO who wouldn't rather have articles written about his company (as long as they are positive) than spend money on advertisements.

This brings to mind the Silly Putty story. In the 1940s, the U.S. War Production Board asked General Electric to make a cheap substitute for rubber that could help with the war effort. James Wright, a GE engineer, produced a synthetic compound he called "nutty putty." In 1949, Paul Hodgson, a former ad copywriter running a toy store, saw a demonstration of the product at a party. Hodgson bought twenty-one pounds of the stuff and hired a Yale student to cut the putty into small balls and place them in small plastic eggs. He called it Silly Putty, and soon it outsold everything else in his little store.

The real stroke of genius here, though, was getting a piece about the Silly Putty in the "Talk of the Town" section of *The New Yorker* magazine, which almost single-handedly launched the huge success of the product in the fifties and sixties.

So, whether you're selling Rollerball pens and using the Israeli Peace Accord as a springboard or you're selling Silly Putty and using magazine articles and word-of-mouth, it is up to your company's PR agency and you as an executive to generate the sizzle necessary to sell your product.

20

Protect Your Name

An Amish man named Smith was injured when he and his horse were struck by a car at an intersection. Smith sued the driver. In court, he was cross-examined by the driver's lawyer.

Lawyer: "Mr. Smith, you've testified all about your injuries. But according to the accident report, you told the investigating officer at the scene that you were not injured. What about that?"

Smith: "Well, let me explain. When the officer arrived at the scene, he first looked at my horse. He said, 'Looks like he has a broken leg.' And then he took out his gun and shot the horse. Then he came up to me and asked how I was doing. I immediately responded, 'I'm fine! I'm fine!'"

Comedians can't resist telling jokes about lawsuits and lawyers—they're such easy targets—and I was no exception. However, as I found from business experience, litigation is no laughing matter.

Among his or her other responsibilities, a good businessperson must be protective of the company's product once it has been distributed and has become part of the consumer's life. Pilot Pen, like other companies with nationwide product distribution, is very conscious of insuring that its name is not used by other commercial enterprises. When 3Com (which used to be U.S. Robotics and is now Palm, Inc.), came out with the Palm Pilot, I knew this name could be quite confusing to consumers; so I decided that some sort of action needed to be taken.

We did not go after them because of the name Pilot. There are a great many companies that use that name. There is a chain of Pilot gas stations, a Pilot Trucking Company, Pilot Life Insurance, Pilot Electronics. And there's nothing we can or really want to do about them. They sell different products than we. However, U.S. Robotics was selling a pocket organizer or PDA (personal digital assistant) that incorporated a writing instrument—a stylus.

We are in the stylus business and we have the necessary trademarks worldwide to insure that we are the only company that markets writing instruments under the name Pilot. On this basis, we wanted to prevent another company from marketing a stylus under our name.

We filed suit in a U.S. court, but the case really ended up being won in a courtroom in France, where they are stricter about using copyrighted names. A judge in Paris ruled that Palm, Inc. couldn't sell its PDA in France with the Pilot name on it, and this decision had a profound impact on the American case. After the French ruling, the Palm, Inc. people decided that if they couldn't sell their product under the name *Palm Pilot* in the large market of France, they might as well change the name globally.

The management at Palm, Inc. changed about two years ago, and soon after, I received a call from their new CEO. He said, "Ron, I'd like to see you."

"For what purpose?" I asked.

"Well," he said, "we'd like to find out how much you would charge us for permission to use the name *Palm Pilot* for our PDA."

I couldn't believe it. We had spent a great deal of money, time, and energy to secure the Pilot name, and here he was trying to get it back.

He went on. "You see, Ron. We've done lots of market research, and it seems like the consumers all agree the name *Palm Pilot* is the best."

I answered, "Sorry, but I can't help you."

"C'mon, Ron, you must have a price. Everybody has a price."

"Not me. There isn't a dollar amount in the world you can offer me. We will not prostitute our good company name."

Taking this trademark dispute to court cost us a good deal in legal fees, but I was adamant about not giving in or changing our tune a few years later. We had worked hard to make the name Pilot synonymous with high quality writing instruments, and I was willing to fight to protect it.

Today Palm, Inc. purchases Pilot stylus products from us for their Palm handheld organizers, proving the old adage that the best way to get even with a (former) adversary is to take his order! Protect your name. It is one of the most important commodities you have.

In commercial life, disputes are commonplace. Most disagreements should be resolved informally, such as by exchange of phone calls or correspondence; but others will require formal proceedings like mediation, arbitration or, as a last resort, litigation. As a high-level executive, it is your job to decide (after consulting legal counsel) whether the dispute is suitable for compromise, or after a lawsuit begins, appropriate for settlement. Just keep uppermost in mind that you cannot and should not be unbending and go running off to court every time someone steps on your toes; you must pick your battles very carefully.

In this respect, don't lose sight of the fact that time spent in giving depositions, for example, is time that otherwise would be used to conduct real business. But when you truly believe that an important principle would be endangered if you failed to take every legal step to protect it, then by all means, stand firm and sue the [expletive deleted].

21

Are You Saying What They're Hearing?

A few years back, one of my older friends began to lose his hearing. We all told him he had to get a hearing aid. For awhile, he didn't want to hear it, but eventually, we were able to persuade him to see his doctor and get fitted with a great hi-tech hearing aid.

A few days later, we were having dinner and he loved his hearing aid so much, he started boasting about it: "This hearing aid is the best ever made. Top of the line, the most advanced model there is. And not cheap either. Very expensive. But it's worth it—I can hear a pin drop!

"That's great!" I told him looking at the tiny contraption in his ear. "What kind is it?"

My friend looked at his watch and said, "Oh, about six-thirty."

Here's another story, a true one, that also involved an "elderly" friend, named Phil. (Actually, I'm a month older than he is, and I'm a young guy.) After a restless night, Phil went to McDonald's for an early breakfast, ordering an Egg McMuffin and a small coffee. The Hispanic woman behind the counter said, "Okay, Egg McMuffin and Señor Coffee."

Phil wondered, was Señor Coffee the Spanish version of the Mr. Coffee that Joe DiMaggio plugged in those old TV commercials? So he asked, "What is Señor Coffee?"

The woman replied, "You know, old coffee."

"Old coffee?" Phil said, "Don't you have any new, fresh coffee?"

She responded, "No, no, Señor means you are old."

Finally the light bulb lit over Phil's sleep-deprived head. She was talk-

ing about senior coffee: coffee McDonald's sells to senior citizens at a discount.

Sheepishly, Phil remarked, "Well, at least you could have asked for my ID," and the small crowd that had gathered by that time broke up with laughter.

When I joined Pilot, I inherited product selling sheets and packaging prepared at our headquarters in Tokyo. Our BP-S Ball Point pen was among these items. The pen has an extremely fine point housed in a stainless steel nose cone. The Marketing Department in Japan wanted to be certain that the consumer was aware of the high quality fine point. To get the message across, they placed on the packaging a cartoon character of a woodpecker with an elongated beak. This intentional exaggeration in the drawing called attention to the point—more so than any other aspect of the pen.

While it is a stick pen, it is also refillable, so a similar cartoon drawing of the woodpecker appeared on the refill packaging. For whatever reason, they proceeded to give the refill a nickname. Unfortunately, the name they chose was "The Pecker." I laughed myself silly the first time I saw it. Eventually, I had to explain to the Japanese staff the meaning of our slang expression, "the pecker." It was quite a discussion, which ultimately dissolved into hysterical laughter and an immediate decision to change the name.

Ironically, the pen and the refill are still best sellers these many years later, and we never did use a nickname. It came to be known as "The Better Ball Point Pen," and it is just that.

These stories speak loudly about the need for clear communication and the ease with which misunderstanding can creep into conversation. This issue of communication and miscommunication became very significant to me when I became the sixth American in history to be elected to the board of directors of any Japanese public company. My elevation to the board couldn't have happened without a mentor at Pilot in Japan, Mr. Akira Tsuneto. Just as Jack Paige was a terrific mentor to me at Bic, I was very fortunate to have someone at our parent company in Tokyo take interest in me.

I've had the pleasure of visiting Japan more than sixty times during my time with Pilot. The Japanese have earned their reputation for being gracious hosts and exceptionally polite people. Unlike let-it-all-hang-out Americans, the Japanese prefer to avoid confrontation and seek agreement.

That is, except for Akira Tsuneto, the former president of Pilot Corporation and the man responsible for my being named a board member. Mr. Tsuneto was direct and to the point. He spoke his mind about what he believed was good for the company.

Japan's centuries of tradition and homogenous population have led to a strong image of what it means to be Japanese. It is highly unusual to meet a Japanese businessman who deviates from what have become cultural characteristics, particularly one over the age of fifty. But Mr. Tsuneto was most unusual. In addition to being candid, he was passionate about hot dogs, Big Band music, and vacationing in France. He didn't smoke. He had lived in Europe. He was proudly Japanese yet he was also a maverick.

For instance, many Japanese companies operate subsidiaries in the United States. Most of them have a Japanese national as the CEO. In 1986, when I was promoted to president, the company's board of directors made the remarkable decision that Pilot Pen Corporation of America would be under my sole leadership. Eventually, we used that management form for our subsidiaries around the world. Today the Pilot operations in England, France, Germany, Hong Kong, Indonesia, Israel, Italy, Malaysia, Russia, and Singapore are run by citizens of those countries, locals who understand the national culture, customs, and market. That autonomy is due to Mr. Tsuneto's willingness to do things differently and to battle for what he believed was right.

Mr. Tsuneto faced some opposition when he stated he wanted me to serve on the Pilot Corporation board of directors. Publicly-held Japanese companies rarely have foreigners serve on their boards. But Mr. Tsuneto was convinced that to be a competitive global company, Pilot must diversify its board. He pushed until it happened: I was elected to the board of directors in March 1992.

Our steadfast public relations man, Jim Plunkett, invested hours poring over the Japan Company Datafile to put my appointment in the context of Americans in leadership roles in Japanese companies. He wrote a news release that the Associated Press picked up and the story shot around the world.

Of course I was thrilled about joining the board of directors and knew it was a great honor. I flew to Tokyo for the Pilot shareholders' meeting, where my directorship was to be confirmed. I assumed it would be like an annual meeting in America. When I walked into the corporate headquarters, I saw a battery of reporters and photographers but thought nothing of it. They were there to cover the meeting. However, as I walked by them, I heard one yell, "There he is!"

Suddenly, as in the movies, this horde of journalists and cameramen from ABC, CNN, and CBS, as well as numerous Japanese stations, ran after me. It was a little scary, let me tell you. (Later, I found out that reporters are not allowed into our shareholders' meetings, so they had to try to interview me outside the meeting room.)

I've studied the Japanese language, but even after years of lessons I have a very limited vocabulary. For that first meeting, I didn't have a translator and had to sit for hours without really understanding what was being said. Occasionally, one of the other directors who was bilingual whispered tidbits of information into my ear.

Since then, I now receive instant translations from two professionals who provide nearly perfect English with an eight- to nine-second delay. As a result, I am now able to participate fully.

I'd like to claim I was elected to the board because of our performance in the United States. By 1992, we'd gone from $1.2 million in sales to $86 million, evidence that I could make some contribution to our global operations. However, I know that despite our performance, none of this would have happened if Mr. Tsuneto's style were less candid. I admired him tremendously for the risks he took to keep Pilot Corporation innovative and competitive in a global market. He showed remarkable courage in his leadership and I am proud to have had him as my friend. Mr. Tsuneto died in 2002.

I learned yet another significant lesson from the Japanese culture and tradition of tolerance.

As president and CEO of Pilot Pen, I was recently asked to become the chairman of a new nonprofit citizens' action group in New Haven, Connecticut, near our corporate headquarters. This group's sole purpose is to advocate improving Tweed-New Haven Regional Airport so small jets can connect New Haven by air to the rest of the nation. I used to be able to fly to Tokyo from Tweed with a connection in Chicago. That airline pulled out of Tweed years ago, forcing tens of thousands of travelers in southern Connecticut to drive to more distant and congested airports on overcrowded highways. Attracting a national carrier back to New Haven would not only give individual travelers back some valuable time, but enhance the region's prospects for economic growth.

As you can imagine, airport expansion appeals to business and pleasure travelers but enrages nearby property owners. As part of its community outreach, this citizens' group scheduled a meeting with homeowners and an antiexpansion organization. I was asked to attend this evening meeting, say a few words about the necessity for expansion, then be free to go home. I was told that while many opponents would be present, there would be a civil, open discussion.

I discovered on entering the meeting room that I was to occupy the center seat at a horseshoe-shaped table, facing several rows of chairs. A few of my fellow members in the proexpansion group joined me at the table, along with leaders of those opposed. Twenty-four people took seats in the rows, crossed their arms over their chests, and glared at me. It quickly became apparent that I was to conduct the meeting and that these homeowners weren't there to politely discuss economic vitality. They didn't want commercial jets landing and taking off in their backyards, period. They were upset and came to vent their frustration.

Did I want to walk out? You bet. But I resolved to salvage what I could and began to build rapport. I calmly explained why I was there and why I believed expansion was necessary. I told them that I wouldn't want to live near an airport either. I asked why they purchased houses in this neighborhood when they knew that an airport was nearby, and listened as identical answers were voiced. In 1983, they said, the mayors of the two towns that govern the airport signed an airport master plan. These homeowners had been led to believe that the plan prohibited any airport expansion. However, the plan had been written in deliberately vague language that allowed broad interpretation. They bought houses thinking they were protected by a document that was now betraying them. No wonder they were incensed! Once the core of their outrage was out in the open and acknowledged, we proceeded with a discussion about property values, business growth, noise pollution, and so on. When the meeting ended, many of them walked up to me to shake my hand.

It had been many decades since my performance at the Coral Gables Veterans Hospital, but that long-ago night put me on a path that enabled me to convert what promised to be a hostile situation into a candid exchange of opinions. We didn't change the world or even our little corner of Connecticut that night, but by the end of the evening, everyone had developed mutual respect, and we all had learned a great deal about each other's situation.

These principles of respect also apply to one-on-one communications. I learned early on that the most important thing I could do was to make sure that the person to whom I was talking felt that I was with him or her in spirit as well as body. I employ this principle every day. This respectful approach helps me build rapport with the other person and encourage deeper levels of communication. I may have a million other things on my mind or may not have gotten any sleep the night before. No matter: I have to make it appear that whatever it is the two of us are talking about at that moment is the most important thing in the world to me. I make direct eye contact, listen carefully to what the person's saying, and always remember that he or she wants my full attention. This is one way people you encounter feel respected; and unless they do, what you say matters little.

I think the most important thing I learned as a comedian was how to connect with others. Whether I had to win over a thousand people in a cavernous auditorium or just sway to my side a single individual in a small lounge, I developed the ability to sell myself—which just may be the most significant factor in any sales pitch.

So whether you are selling jokes, pens, a point of view, or anything else, sales success is about first endowing people with confidence in yourself. How do you do that? You believe in yourself and your ability to sell. How? You maintain a relaxed, confident demeanor. How? Through belief in the value of your product and extensive preparation of your sales approach. How? By thorough knowledge of your product and your customer. And I cannot overemphasize that your dealings with the customer, or anyone else for that matter, must be respectful.

Clear and unambiguous communication is essential to conducting corporate business, particularly when different languages and cultures are involved. A single mishandled word can change the entire substance of a message. It also is essential, particularly in potentially hostile circumstances, that viewpoints be exchanged in a respectful manner, and a sincere attempt be made to understand and appreciate opposing positions. Where compromise is appropriate, it cannot be forged on a foundation of discord.

22

Show Business Secrets for Presentations

When I was in Paris many years ago, I thought I spotted Picasso at an out-door café, drinking coffee and reading the paper. An older woman approached him and asked in an American accent, "Excuse me, you're Picasso, aren't you?"

He put down his paper, looked over the top of his reading glasses, and said, "Yes, Madam, I am."

She held out a piece of paper and said, "I thought so! Would you draw a picture?"

He obliged her request and sketched something while she watched. She was delighted with the result and asked if she could have it.

"Of course, Madam," replied Picasso. "That will be five thousand dollars."

"Five thousand dollars!" she exclaimed. "Why, that drawing only took you a few seconds!"

"No, Madam," he replied. "That drawing took fifty-two years."

This emphasis on perceived value reminds me of a story that concerns my son, Steve, when he was about twelve years old and on his summer vacation. I thought this would be a perfect opportunity for us to spend some time together, so I invited him to travel with me to Philadelphia where I was scheduled to speak to a large sales and marketing association. Steve agreed and we drove from Connecticut to Pennsylvania together.

When we arrived at the hotel where the conference was taking place, Steve and I found a ballroom filled to capacity with businesspeople anxious to hear what I had to say. As we walked in, I remember Steve looking over at me and saying, "Jeez, Dad, are all these people really here to listen to you?"

I laughed and nodded yes.

Then he added, "I hope you tell them some jokes that are better than the ones you use at home."

Filled with confidence from my son's big pep talk, I ascended to the podium and began by telling one of my favorite jokes. However, I didn't tell the audience that I was telling them a joke. I let them discover that for themselves as I went along, and I was soon rewarded for my choice when the ballroom filled with laughter.

The next day, we were back in the car driving home. Steve looked over at me and said, "Dad, I can't believe there were people there who actually paid twenty-five dollars to listen to you tell the same stories you tell us around the dinner table for free."

I laughed again. "Yep. I guess I'm going to have to charge you guys for dinnertime conversation from now on."

Steve laughed, "Dad, there's one other thing I want to ask you."

"Shoot."

"These people just paid money to hear all about the secrets to your success, and you spoke for forty minutes, but still, it seemed like all you did was just tell a few jokes and a bunch of stories."

I looked over at him and said, "Yes, but the important thing is, those few jokes and stories might be all they needed to hear to succeed!"

Just as Picasso was paid for a lifetime of work even if what he drew only took a few minutes, I was being received as a speaker for a lifetime of knowledge accumulated in the business world. People will always come to hear speakers who they think have something of value to impart that might be directly helpful to them. But whether a speaker retains or loses the audience depends greatly upon his or her projection of self-confidence in delivering the message; and self-confidence is grounded in thorough preparation and belief in the positive value of the message. Because value can be a function of perception, then that perception starts from how one values him- or herself. In turn, that value is a quality that will be evident in any speech you give or public presentation you make.

Thinking about the numerous speaking engagements I have accepted, there are a host of techniques and lessons I've learned from masterful performers in show business. The key is that memorable presentations blend great content with great theater. Anyone can become a polished performer by following these same principles and investing time in rehearsal.

Your Staging

If you will be on a theatrical-style stage, with lighting and offstage wings, you'll have the best resources available to you. If you'll be speaking from a tabletop podium in a banquet room as people eat lunch, you can still employ aspects of these techniques for a powerful presentation.

No matter what type of staging you encounter, the lighting and sound system are critical. After years of working in nightclubs, I noticed that the major performers have very strong opinions about how they should be lit. You should be just as detail-oriented. If you'll be presenting in a banquet hall or conference room, you can build drama with a fixed floodlight attached to the ceiling and directed at you (there are portable floods with clamps that are ideal for temporary lighting). Check if the room lighting can be dimmed. If you'll be referring to notes, make sure the podium light works.

Check the sound system and any audio-visual equipment a few hours before your audience arrives. Test your microphone. How close to your mouth does it need to be? If it's handheld, that frees you to move around during your presentation and gives your hands a prop.

Quick Tip: Listen to the microphone's amplification of your first few words once you start your presentation. Despite thorough sound checks, the sound system may need readjustment once the room is filled.

Theater-Style Stage. Think drama and mystique. You want the house lights down, leaving the audience sitting in darkness and focusing on you in the spotlight. Position your podium in the center, within inches of the front of the stage. You want to build intimacy with your audience and your proximity to them is essential. Work with the lighting technician to follow your entrance, presentation, and exit with a spotlight.

Conference Hall or Banquet Room. If you'll be speaking while your audience is eating a meal, make sure that the tables are set up so close to the stage or speaker's podium that there is only enough room for the waiters to squeeze through. The tables in the room should be just as close to each other. Again, you want to create a warm, friendly atmosphere where intimacy is possible. This closeness has a huge impact on the way your presentation is perceived. If moving the tables forward and near each other leaves an intolerable amount of bare space in the room, ask the facility manager to disguise it with plants, screens, or some other visual fillers. When your audience will be sitting in chairs and not at tables, apply the same philosophy. Move the chairs close to you.

Crowd-Control Tip

The easiest way to get an audience quiet is to turn out the lights and put a spotlight on the person speaking. If a theatrical spotlight is not available, at the very least make sure there is some type of light to illuminate the speaker while the room is in darkness.

Your Introduction

Write your own introduction and give it to the person who will be introducing you. Keep it short and relevant to your audience (no lengthy resume!). Reserve the mention of your name until the very end. In show business, the masters know to build anticipation to create audience excitement. Just as a stripper doesn't begin her act naked and a comedian doesn't lead with a punch line, your introduction should stimulate your audience's imagination.

Think of the thrill of being in a room as someone stands and says, "Tonight's speaker has enjoyed unrivaled access to the leaders of countries and industries around the globe. This evening our guest will talk about his [her] primary concerns and hopes for our country over the next four years, and what those mean to each of you. Ladies and gentlemen, may I present the President of the United States."

I actually had the privilege of introducing former President Gerald Ford, and a definite shiver of excitement flashed through the room when I ended my introduction with his name. When composing your introduction, build audience anticipation with your credentials and what your topic means to members of your audience, saving your name until the end.

Your Entrance

Of course, you are impeccably groomed and dressed appropriately for your audience. If you're presenting from a theatrical stage, use it for a theatrical entrance from the wings. Otherwise, simply move into position at the podium after you've been introduced.

Once you've made your entrance, launch straight into what you have to say. Don't dilute the impact of your opening with thanking your hosts or remarking how great it is to be in that city. Think of the first few seconds of a film. Would James Bond look into the camera and say, "Good evening. Thanks for buying a movie ticket!"?

If you're a panelist on a dais, don't feel compelled to introduce everyone, especially if they will eventually speak and be introduced later. The only people you could introduce are those who are not speaking and would otherwise not be mentioned. If you must introduce the people on the dais, avoid the cliché "From my right and your left...." As with other introductions, reserve the speaker's name until the end.

Your Presentation

Opening. As a comedian, I learned to open with my strongest material. It was a sure way to connect with the audience, reassure them that they could relax with me, and help me to relax into my act. The audience was prepared for comedy and that's what I delivered. Your audience is anticipating your message, so please don't feel obliged to begin your presentation with a joke. If you're exceptionally skilled at telling jokes, then pick an appropriate one and have fun. But learn from the pros, as I did. When you are going to tell a joke, don't let people know it's a joke before you tell it. If you don't feel comfortable about telling a joke, then don't! Trust me, it's better to not even attempt a joke than to tell one poorly and launch your presentation with a giant thud.

Every comedian, every actor, and every speaker is nervous when walking onstage. That adrenaline rush can make relaxing impossible. That's why the pros have learned to act as if they're relaxed. To help you pretend to be at ease, prepare like the pros do. Do your homework. Make sure you know your subject and you've rehearsed. These preparations will give you confidence; and gaining confidence will lessen your tension, helping you to transform your relaxation act into the real thing. When you appear to be at ease and begin with your strongest material, your audience will respond favorably. This chain reaction will result in your genuinely relaxing and having a great time.

Notes. Whenever I speak in public presentations, I write brief notes on the back of an envelope. I've seen other speakers use index cards. I like to work with key words and phrases so that one glance will trigger a section of my speech. If you work with notes, allow ample time for rehearsal—not to memorize your speech word-for-word, but to imprint the sequence of your presentation's stories, facts, and insights into your mind. Select key words or phrases to represent each section and rehearse some more, referring only to your key words. By the time you give your speech, you may not need to refer to your notes at all. (I refer to my notes up to the time of my introduction, and then tuck them in the breast pocket of my jacket right before I speak.) Your audience will respond to you as if you are speaking extemporaneously, even though you are presenting prepared and rehearsed material. After your speech, if some special phrasing or powerful concept came up during your talk that got a good response, write it down so you can include it in your next presentation.

Audience Connection. Unlike one-on-one communication, you don't need to make eye contact with people in your audience. Instead, slowly pan the room, turning your face and attention to address those areas where people are seated. When it's appropriate to what you're saying, smile. Relax your facial muscles. Gesture naturally. Be yourself. Remember, you are talking to an ideal audience—a roomful of people who want you to succeed!

Closing. Just as you started with your strongest material, end with strong material. Never close by saying "And in conclusion…." This is a sure way of telling the audience you were boring. Close with a great line or a memorable point that sums up the essence of your message.

Your Exit

Before you get onstage or step to the podium, know where your exit is. When you've finished your presentation, accept the applause. Stand tall, smile, and bask in that wave of appreciation. You've earned it! If there is no question-and-answer session following your speech, make your exit before the applause dies down. If there is a Q & A session, make sure everyone hears the question (repeat it for the audience or use a roving handheld microphone) and make sure you understand it before answering. Keep your answers thoughtful and succinct, and don't be embarrassed to say you don't know the answer.

Media Interviews

When doing any media interview, you want to combine sounding and looking confident with being relaxed. Concentrate on the reporter. For broadcast interviews, don't be concerned about the microphone or camera. Strive to be the same person you are when you're talking with your best friend. Be upbeat, use the reporter's name, and smile (if appropriate to the nature of the interview). If you use humor, use the self-deprecating kind. Tell stories that show your humanity or reveal a valuable lesson you've learned.

Come to the interview prepared. Know the angle of the story, some background information on the reporter, and who the readers, listeners, or viewers are. You'll find that when you're interviewed, different reporters will often ask you the same questions. Prepare succinct, clearly thought-out answers. Don't attempt to come up with fresh responses to the same questions when you already have good answers at your command.

Even though the reporter asks the questions, always include your message in your answers (you see some politicians doing this to the point that they completely ignore the question). If you have a key point you want to make about your company, product, or cause, weave it into your answers.

Characterize your responses with attention getters such as "The biggest mistake," "The most interesting aspect," or "The three most important points are…" Use dramatic action verbs and, instead of generalities, specific facts and figures. Include anecdotes to illustrate a point. If you don't know the answer to a question, admit it instead of faking it. And it is always better to pause for a second than to say, "Um" or "Well…"

Briefly pausing before responding also helps you to ensure you understand each question. If you have any uncertainty, either request that the question be repeated, or say, "As I understand it, you are asking…," and then state the question as you believe you heard it.

Take every interview seriously, no matter how small the publication or program may be. You never know who may be reading, listening, or watching. If media interviews are a regular part of your job, work with a media trainer so you can take maximum advantage of these opportunities.

When you're addressing business people, your appearance greatly affects how you are received and your ability to convince them you mean business. It's not coincidence that the root of "addressing" is "dress."

I've always emphasized to my children and my employees that no matter what they do in life, they should never do it halfway. Recently when I was speaking with my son, Steve, who is now a successful video director/producer, he reminded me of when he was growing up and we were having financial difficulties. He remembers how I tried to drive a nice car, dress in good clothes, and always be impeccably groomed. He remembers me telling him that, "If you look the part, doors will open that might otherwise remain closed. After that, it will be up to you to prove you deserve to stay there."

Call me old-fashioned, but I've always been a firm believer in the adage: clothes make the woman or man. Let's face it, first impressions count. And inevitably, you will be judged not just on how well you make your presentation, but also on how you look. So, please, don't overlook wardrobe. I am partial to a crisp appearance. For men in business, shirts need to be the proper collar size, and about one-quarter inch of cuff should show past the jacket sleeve. Suits should be properly tailored, and trousers shouldn't bunch up around the ankles. Ties should be properly knotted. For women, skirts should not be too short. For men and women, nails should be manicured and hair should be neatly trimmed. Shoes should always be shined.

If you want to be taken seriously, let people know you take yourself seriously by presenting yourself with care. Especially with the rise of dress-down days, casual Fridays, and differing dress codes, appearance can be the key to how people perceive you. Give it your all. Make the effort to look good and speak well. You won't be sorry you did.

23

Listen to Your Instincts

A friend of mine recently retired and finally fulfilled his dream of running a sheep ranch. One day he was overseeing his grazing flock when a new, fancy sport utility vehicle crested the hill and stopped beside him in a cloud of dust. Out climbed an impeccably dressed man in a perfectly tailored suit who walked up to my friend.

"Shepherd," the stranger said, addressing my friend, "if I can guess how many sheep you have grazing on this hillside, will you give me one of your animals?"

Stunned by his bravado, my friend said yes.

The stranger opened the passenger door, set up a laptop and portable printer, aimed an antenna skyward and hooked up to a satellite that beamed down on the flock. He worked the keyboard and within a few moments printed out a twenty-seven-page report with color charts. The stranger placed the report in a folder, presented it to my friend, and announced, "Shepherd, you have 1,638 sheep grazing in your flock today."

My friend looked at him in astonishment and said that was precisely correct! Whereupon the stranger swept up one of the animals and put it in the back of his vehicle. As he was about to drive off, my friend called out "Sir, I have a proposition for you. If I can guess your occupation, may I have my animal back?"

Stunned himself, the stranger replied, "All right."

Without hesitation my friend announced, "You're a consultant."

The stranger's jaw dropped, then he asked, "How did you know?"

My friend said, "There are three reasons. First, you stuck your nose into my business uninvited. Second, it's clear that you know nothing about me or my business. Third, you better take my dog out of your truck!"

It's tempting to turn to outside professionals who promise they can provide insights into your business. Sometimes their fresh perspectives can uncover overlooked opportunities. However, examples abound of companies that relied on "experts" to expand their businesses in places they did not belong. So that I will never forget this, I carry three famous market research reports with me: the reports on the Edsel, New Coke, and Real cigarettes. For each of these products, more research was done in their respective product categories than had ever before been done. Ford invested a record amount of money in research to bring us the Edsel, which failed miserably. Coke, the leader in the soft drink world, spent a fortune on research for New Coke—and what happened? It was instantly rejected. R.J. Reynolds spent millions on researching why the so-called "healthy" cigarette—the Real cigarette—couldn't fail and yet, IT FLOPPED!

In the end, the only people who made money from each of these new products were the research companies who convinced a few insecure CEOs that they had to be armed with piles of papers and statistics before they walked into their boardrooms and pitched their new product ideas to their boards. Sure, sometimes research is helpful, but in general I believe it is a CEO's job to rely on feel-and-touch instinct. There is always the chance of a flop, and nobody can have a perfect track record with every product; but businesspeople must never get so caught up in their research that they lose touch with their own instincts. Scan the research if you feel so compelled, but in the end, go with your instincts—they put you where you are.

Indeed, any truly honest businessman will admit that no matter what the research says, nobody can know for sure how any product will sell. In 1973, for example, Xerox Corporation had the ALTO personal computer with user interface complete with windows and icons. It even had a primitive plug-in mouse. Xerox also had developed software that allowed the user to do word processing, spreadsheets, and desktop publishing.

But the people at Xerox failed to see the value of these products and didn't pursue them. Instead, they stayed focused on copying machines. Meanwhile, Apple's Steve Jobs made a fortune by capitalizing on the icon and window concepts and incorporating them into Apple products. Bill Gates's Microsoft Corporation ended up with all the word processing software rights incorporated now into Microsoft Word.

It's simple to look at Xerox in retrospect and wonder how they could have fumbled so badly. It's easy to say they mismanaged or should have marketed their products differently. But in 1973, they saw their future in copying machines and not personal computers, and thus, they thought it would be more financially viable to pursue that portion of the industry.

Most companies are like Xerox in that regard. There is only a limited amount of money available for marketing. Corporate leaders and bean counters must determine where to push those funds and ad dollars, and all the while, everyone is praying they've made the right choices and pushed in the right direction.

At Pilot, we are in the same situation. Now take our Razor Point pens—please! (My apologies to the great comedian Henny Youngman.) They are huge sellers in America, but were a big flop in Canada. How do you explain that? To be honest, we can't. We have just accepted these market realities and we acted accordingly. But don't forget that Razor Point's American success began with an advertising campaign that defied traditional thinking. We went forward with it because our instincts told us it would generate a winner. So too does the Dr. Grip success story (in an upcoming chapter) validate our reliance on our instincts that an unconventional launch would work.

So, if you have the opportunity to make marketing decisions, remember that regardless of any market research and statistics, it's your job that is on the line, and you have to obey your gut instincts to either forge ahead or sit tight. If you know your industry, go with what you know and fight for what you believe in.

24

Marketing Hidden Treasures

A professional golfer was sitting in the bar at his club one day, when a blind man came up to sit next to him. He was puzzled to see the man in the bar. He seemed to be on his own, so the pro golfer, feeling sorry for him, bought him a drink. "Are you waiting for someone?"

"No," replied the man, "I'm a member here."

The pro golfer couldn't hide his disbelief and rudely exclaimed, "But how can you play golf? You're blind!"

The man smiled and explained, "I get my caddie to walk down the fairway and call to me. Then I hit the ball in the direction of his voice."

"That's amazing!" said the pro. "But how do you putt?"

"Easy," replied the blind man, "I get my caddie to lie down behind the hole with his head on the ground and I just play the ball towards his voice."

The golfer was overwhelmed by all of this and asked the blind man if he had a handicap. "Actually," the man said, "I'm a scratch golfer."

The golfer couldn't contain his curiosity. "I'd love to see you play," he said. "Perhaps you'd like to play a round with me sometime."

"I only play for money," warned the blind man. "And it's got to be a thousand dollars a hole!"

The golf pro laughed, but he could also see the blind man was serious. In the end, not really wanting to offend the man, the pro agreed.

"Great!" said the blind man. "What night would you like to play?"

D on't rush into judging other people or products. You can never be too sure of anything. Sometimes you just have to have the flexibility to reevaluate what the best business applications really are for a product. Many times a great product or employee may already be part of your company; you just have to see how to apply and market them. Silly Putty and the Razor Point pen exemplify this principle, as do the Dr. Grip pen and the Pilot product called Magna Doodle, the world's most popular drawing toy.

The Dr. Grip story and the Dr. Grip pen itself are prime examples of "non-convention." The prototype for the pen was developed in 1991 by Hiroshi Udo, a Japanese physician who designed it for use by people with arthritic hands. Pilot Corporation secured a license from Dr. Udo to produce and sell the pen, but it was launched only in Japan, where it sold in modest numbers. I brought Dr. Grip samples back to the U.S., but decided not to market the pen here because I thought it was ugly (too fat), too expensive, and just had a "bad" name to sell well in America. However, over the next couple of years, the Japanese sales figures kept improving, so I determined to advertise and sell the pen in the U.S. at a price even higher than in Japan. I took this action despite not knowing exactly *why* it was succeeding in Japan, despite our marketing department's view that the price was too high, and despite the absence of distribution channels when the Dr. Grip TV commercial was aired. We thus began to sell the Dr. Grip by bucking all conventional marketing wisdom. We needed a quick commercial success, and I thought Dr. Grip represented our best shot.

Fortunately, the TV commercial, which showed me as a small figure in a pen user's shirt pocket, had a great positive impact, generating demand well beyond arthritis sufferers. The Dr. Grip has continued to surprise us: it is a big seller in college bookstores, whose young patrons have virtually no physical problems with their hands. We have expanded it to six versions, including a gel pen and a mechanical pencil; and received a commendation from the Arthritis Foundation, an exclusive honor we are permitted to cite in advertising. Although I didn't like its name or its shape, or that distribution arrangements were not timely in place, good markets emerged for the unconventional Dr. Grip pen.

Magna Doodle was invented in 1974 by a group of engineers working for our parent company. They were assigned to design a dustless chalkboard for business applications. When a member of the Takara Toy Company was visiting Pilot and accidentally saw the prototype, he asked if he could place an order. He was told that the prototype he was looking at was no toy. It was a business tool with a cost per unit of more than $25, which was much too expensive for a toy. The Takara Toy employee soon left, but his idea for a magnetic-screen toy took hold. Our company immediately formed a project team to develop a means to mass-produce the product at a much more affordable level, and soon the Magna Doodle was born.

The product was first marketed in Japan and almost instantly became a big hit. In the mid-1980s, we wanted to bring it to America, but we realized we needed the trade connections of a strong toy company to bring it into the homes of American families nationwide. So in 1986, we chose View-Master to launch the market line.

Tyco Toys acquired View-Master in 1989 and launched Magna Doodle's first television advertising campaign in the spring of 1990. Under Tyco's direction, Magna Doodle achieved one sales record after another despite stiff competition. Five years later, Tyco and Pilot celebrated the manufacturing of our 40 millionth Magna Doodle. Magna Doodle, with its emphasis on ease of use, imagination, creativity, and fun, consistently outsells every other toy in the mechanical design category. Almost half of the households in America with children under seven years of age own a Magna Doodle and over 80 million have been sold.

In 1997, Mattel, Inc. acquired Tyco Toys, and Magna Doodle moved to Mattel's Fisher-Price division. Soon after, Fisher-Price began to restyle the entire Magna Doodle line to assure its continued success into the twenty-first century. The new styles incorporate handles and clips for conveniently taking Magna Doodle from place to place. Today's versions include the regular, deluxe, travel, and pocket clip-on Magna Doodle.

In the spring of 2004, we formed a new partnership with Ohio Art Company, the makers of Etch A Sketch. Ohio Art will now be the exclusive distributor of Magna Doodle, thus bringing the two leading magnetic drawing toys together. Even with Magna Doodle's great success, we haven't sat on our laurels. Other products that incorporate the magnetic screen technology include the QUEST,™ a device that allows divers to communicate underwater; the Clean Mag, that allows for use in sterile business environments; and the Mag Media, for use in stadiums, schools, and other public places.

Ever since I sat atop my first Schwinn Black Phantom bicycle, I've been drawn to and felt the power of doing things right, of going all out. Treat yourself like the best, and you will become the best. Cut corners, and it shows. These truisms became apparent to me when we first started considering the marketing of Pilot's high-end writing instruments that are now known as Namiki. These pens range from the $125 Vanishing Point, the world's only one-click retractable fountain pen, to our top-of-the-line Namiki, which costs $6,500. Usually this pen is purchased not for writing, but by collectors to be kept under glass as a work of art. Many of these high-end pens are finished with a special Japanese process known as *Maki-e* (pronounced MOCK-ee-ay). This process endows the most expensive Namiki writing instruments with a gorgeous, highly lacquered artistic finish. All illustrations on the bodies of these pens are done by hand by artists with brushes so small that some have only two rat-hair bristles.

Back in the 1970s, our high-end writing instruments were

not called Namikis; they were just very expensive Pilot pens. This, however, eventually resulted in some problems. For example, imagine two big business executives who are about to sign an important agreement that they've spent months negotiating. One of the executives whips out his $3,000 Pilot fountain pen he's purchased for just such a special occasion. Then his counterpart pulls out his black seventy-nine cent Pilot disposable pen. At this point, one would tend to believe that the businessman who had just spent $3,000 on a Pilot pen might feel a little foolish.

When you are dealing with high-end products like very expensive pens, there is a distinct snob appeal that must be taken into consideration. Thus, I determined that we needed to shut down Pilot's high-end pen distribution in North America in the late seventies, and I promised our Japanese parent company that we would reopen it in a year or two once we had made some very specific marketing decisions.

My time estimate was off the mark by only a decade; we ended up taking eleven years before bringing our high-end writing instruments back into the North American market. And when we did, we knew the most important thing was that these pens must not be known as Pilot. They had to have a name that rang with distinction—something that would carry the same prestige as a name like Tiffany. As luck would have it, a fascinating cultural occurrence took place during the intervening eleven years. America had shifted 180 degrees in how Japanese products were regarded.

In other words, during the seventies some Japanese products were still seen as lacking good quality, but by the late eighties, Japanese products had become known as the epitome of good quality.

So we decided to lean towards a Japanese name—but what would it be? Many possibilities were bandied about the office until somebody in our marketing department suggested going with the original name of our company in 1918—Namiki. It sounded great, so we did an investigation into the Namiki name only to find out that over the years another company had bought the rights. So we bought back the name. Once we finally secured the legal rights to the Namiki name, we spent a great deal of time designing a logo and attractive gift boxes to present the pens. Every eighteen months, we sell a specially designed model as a signed and numbered limited edition of only seven hundred pens worldwide. Today, collectors and true pen lovers can purchase Namiki pens all across America, wherever fine pens are sold.

Aesthetics matter, whether the subject is a pen, a Black Phantom bicycle, or you. If you want to write, you don't need to spend hundreds or thousands of dollars for a pen. You can buy our BetterGrip ballpoint for seventy-nine cents. There are many people who purchase our Namiki pens, however, simply because they are beautiful. In addition to being fine writing instruments, they are an accessory, like a fine watch or expensive jewelry. They let you express yourself by what you write and by the artistry of the pen itself. Sure, physical appearance isn't everything; the pens must write well—there must be substance beneath the surface. But in the end, as any retailer will tell you, most sales usually result from customers being drawn to physical appearances first. Customers come back because, after being hooked by appearances, they are then pleased with performance; but remember, it was the appearance that hooked them initially.

As you go about your management job, take some time to examine critically the physical appearance of your products and their packaging. Although aesthetic judgment is inherently subjective, you will know whether they have a positive or negative impact on you. Then seek opinions from others, especially retailers and customers. If their reactions are no better than lukewarm, ask whoever is responsible for design how improvements might be made. In this, or similar manner, you may be able to turn a liability into an asset, because appearance and packaging do sell products.

These principles apply to your printed promotional materials as well as to what you are selling. Whether you are marketing services, products, or both, all your brochures, web sites, video proposals, correspondence on letterhead, indeed anything bearing your business name, should be designed, crafted, and written with attention to appearance. Also, whether these items are prepared by you, or by others within or outside your organization, make sure a good proofreader/fact checker reviews everything. Misspelled words, typographical errors, and substantive mistakes, for example, can do more harm than just ruining or diminishing an otherwise beautiful presentation. Because mistakes and errors demonstrate sloppiness, people encountering your materials easily make the jump to suspicion that similar carelessness affects how your products are made, your services provided, and your organization run.

Like it or not, you get judged on the appearance of what you put forward—including your personal appearance, as I discussed earlier. Suffice to say now that each time you meet face-to-face with a potential customer, you have the opportunity to complement, rather than detract from, all those aesthetically appealing promotional materials your organization went to such great lengths to perfect.

25

Pay Attention to the Big Rocks

I was in a time-management course once where I learned a valuable lesson. The instructor used an illustration to open the seminar that I will never forget. He stood in front of the class and put a huge glass jar on the table in front of him. He then took a bag of rocks from under his desk and started filling the jar with them. When he could fit no more rocks in, he stood back and asked the class, "Is the jar full?"

"Yes!" we all answered immediately. He shook his head and reached under his desk and pulled out a bag of gravel. He poured the gravel into the jar and the stones began to slip down and fill the spaces between the rocks. "Now is the jar full?" he asked. Aware that this was another trick question, most of us remained silent.

Someone spoke up from the back row. "Probably not," he said.

"Good!" the instructor exclaimed. He now produced a bucket of sand from under his desk and proceeded to pour sand into the jar, which took up the tiny spaces between the pieces of gravel and the rocks. "Is it full now?" he asked.

"No!" we all replied, having caught on to his game. He nodded his head, picked up the pitcher of water on his desk and poured it into the jar until it spilled over the brim. He then looked up at us and said, "Now the jar is full. What is the point of this illustration?"

I raised my hand and said with admiration for his little demonstration, "You're illustrating that no matter how full your schedule is, there's always room to fit more in if you try."

I sat back smugly, expecting to be congratulated for my interpretation.

But the instructor shook his head. "No," he said. "The illustration shows us that if you don't put the big rocks in first, you'll never get them all in."

W hat are the big rocks in your life? Your family? Your health? Your education? Your dreams? Your favorite causes?

Whatever your big rocks are, make sure you put them into your life first. If you fill your life with the smaller stuff of lesser importance (like the sand and the gravel), you'll never fit in the more important things. Sometimes, however, outside forces will change the nature of the rocks, and you'll have to accommodate those changes. Besides working on a personal level, this lesson can also be applied on a corporate, and even global, level. In fact, in the eighties, I saw how America seemed to be putting its little rocks in first, and I spoke up about it.

If you remember, the 1980s marked a moment in history when a wave of protectionism against foreign products swept across the nation. Also at this time it seemed as if Japan could eclipse the United States in economic wealth and manufacturing power. In an effort to combat this new "foreign threat," the U.S. government decided to try to step in and "protect" its economy. I was then COO of Pilot—the American subsidiary of a Japanese corporation. I had divided loyalties and was a bit uncertain exactly how I should proceed.

But I did know this for sure: As a loyal American, I want the freedom of choice to buy the best product, wherever it is made, and I do not like the idea of being told what I can and cannot sell here in the United States. The whole concept of curtailing free trade always had bothered me. I also thought these new protectionist threats did not serve America's economy, but in fact were counterproductive. The one thing I did know was that we couldn't afford to wait and see in which direction the American economic and political winds would blow.

Yet, all the threats against so-called foreign products seemed vague until one day, a member of the U.S. Congress wandered into the office supply store in the basement of the House of Representatives in Washington. This congressman was appalled by all the non-American-made products on display. In a huff, he ran to the floor of Congress where he delivered a fervent speech about the evils of foreign-made products. Now, needless to say, Pilot had quite a presence in this stationery store, and so I was personally affronted by this attack.

In fact, just a week before his tirade, there was a photo in *Time* magazine of First Lady Rosalynn Carter holding a Pilot pen in her hand, and things were really starting to look up for us. So the idea of our product being banished from U.S. soil because a single member of Congress didn't like the fact that there were more "Japanese" pens being sold in his stationery store than "American" pens was very scary to me. It was true at that time that every Pilot pen sold in America was made in Japan. Yet, we were a U.S.-based company, and I didn't believe that the point of origin of any product for which the designated customs tariff had been paid justified a ban against the product.

By this time, we had moved our headquarters to Port Chester, New York, and I got in touch with our congressman. I told him how upset I was and how I wanted a chance to give my side of the story. He agreed to meet with me, and I flew to Washington, D.C. Without getting too emotional, I forcefully told him something like this: "There really isn't a funnel that runs under the Pacific Ocean from Japan and comes up in the stationery store in the basement of the House of Representatives. Even though our Pilot pens are manufactured in Japan, we ship them to the United States by boat where we pay U.S. customs duties. Then, our pens are taken off the boats by American longshoremen, and the containers are placed on flatbed trucks driven by American Teamsters Union members. Then, they are brought to our American warehouse where we employ only American workers, and then they are packaged and shipped around the country on American trucks to American stores with American salespeople, and sold by advertisements written by American admen to be published in American magazines."

My entire speech clearly demonstrated to him that any easy delineation of the evils of foreign-made products being sold in the United States was a vast oversimplification.

And it worked.

Our representative took the floor and convinced Congress to back off. The U.S. government didn't carry out its threat to ban the importation of Japanese-made products. But we at Pilot Pen Corporation of America were able to read the writing on the wall. This threat was a good kick in the pants to accelerate plans we'd already been making to open manufacturing facilities in North America.

In 1985, for the first time in the sixty-seven-year history of Pilot, we started assembling Japanese ballpoint pens in the United States. We had determined that making pens in the United States allowed us to respond more quickly to changing market needs. Also, without the import fees, we could offer our products at lower prices over the long run, which more than justified the initial capital costs of building additional facilities.

In the end, this chain of events was fortuitous. We are now able to control our own destiny, and we no longer have, literally, to wait for the boat to come in. The importation-ban threat, which could have badly hurt business, instead aided us. It forced me to confront a new bully. Instead of getting cuts and bruises, we opened our manufacturing facilities here in North America and released Pilot America from total dependency on foreign shipments.

It sometimes happens that external events change your priorities involuntarily. To adapt to those changes, or better yet, turn them to your advantage, you must modify your business plan strategies. By incorporating measures, including available leverage, to deal with unforeseen occurrences, you ensure your ability to put the big rocks in first.

26

Fanatical Customer Service

An old friend of mine, Irwin Helford, went through a series of promotions similar to mine, and one geographic move, to achieve great success as the CEO of Viking Office Products. As a young man in 1956, Irwin fell into the office supply industry right out of the Navy, joining a company in Chicago called Wilson Jones, then a manufacturer of many best-selling office products. At Wilson Jones, Irwin worked in shipping, customer service, and sales.

In 1960, the Reliable Stationery Company hired him as general manager to develop a new catalog and direct its mail-marketing program. He was also responsible for operations, the sales force, and telephone sales. At this time, Reliable's revenues were $700,000 a year. As Reliable's catalog sales started to take off, Irwin was promoted to vice president of marketing.

Twenty-three years later, under Irwin's leadership, Reliable's annual revenues were up to $40 million. In 1983, he was recruited away from Chicago by Los Angeles-based Viking Office Products. At the time, Viking's sales were stagnant at $15 million a year. Irwin had been living all his life in Chicago and never planned on moving. For years, Reliable and Viking has been friendly competitors; but when Viking offered him complete authority to run the company, Irwin couldn't resist the challenge. So, he pulled up roots and moved to California.

Irwin joined Viking as president and later became CEO and

chairman. He created all new merchandising, catalogs, distribution systems, and a radically innovative "Fanatical Customer Service" concept. Working with a great Viking team, Irwin pushed sales to $1.4 billion in 1997. In August 1998, Viking merged with Office Depot to form the world's largest distributor of office products, with combined revenues of $9 billion in nineteen countries. By the year 2000, Office Depot generated nearly $12 billion in revenues, including about $2 billion from its Viking subsidiary.

Irwin attributes Viking's phenomenal success to no single grand vision, but he can isolate three crucial factors. First, Viking committed to "Fanatical Customer Service," which did not exist in the office supply business before. "Fanatical Customer Service" simply means always doing more than the customer expects: no back orders, no substitutions, no mistakes, no misleading promises, and free same-day delivery for every order in twenty-one major U.S. and eleven overseas cities, and overnight delivery anywhere else. Viking's goal is to impress customers so much that they want to buy from Viking again. In other words, Viking aims to shock customers with its high level of service. As a result, Viking might not have the lowest prices in the industry, but they have the highest customer retention of any office supply company. And now with the rise of Internet sales, Viking is reaching even more customers.

The second key factor is Viking's extraordinary catalogs. The company now has no salesmen and no retail stores. Sales are generated purely by catalog marketing. At any given time, Viking offers dozens of different catalogs targeted at different market segments. Since 1984, its marketing team has developed databases that capture everything about its customers, including brand preferences, the equipment they use, how many times a year they order, and so on. Thanks to inkjet imaging, digital technology, and full-color printing, Viking can now custom print most of its catalogs. The buyer's name is incorporated directly into the copy, and the customized catalog features products Viking believes that customer will want at prices designed to trigger an order. As a result, even though it mails millions of catalogs, Viking still focuses on one customer at a time. That's what I call "Fanatical Customer Service."

Along the same lines, but smaller scale, is another Razor Point story. I like to read the letters we receive from customers so I can be attuned to their requests and frustrations. One customer gave me a strong reminder of how attached people become to our pens. Though our Razor Point pen is no longer our best seller, we continue to manufacture it because it has such strong brand loyalty. However, we decided to limit distribution of the red ink version. Before too long, I received a scathing letter from a customer who used a red ink Razor Point every day to do *The New York Times* crossword puzzle. I immediately sent him a dozen red-ink Razor Points and was reminded of the loyalty our pens command.

The (Razor) point here is to listen to your customers. It costs little or nothing to do so, you can find out directly what they will or won't buy, and through their appreciation of knowing you actually heed their comments, achieves the kind of loyalty that only thoughtful service inspires.

The final element Irwin finds essential is the people he hires. He ensures that the company hired only particular kinds of people. If prospective hires couldn't demonstrate a deep caring for the customer, they were not Viking material. The company has no personnel or human resource department—the division in charge of hiring and firing is called the People Department. And once it hires someone, no matter at what level, the company shows great devotion to him or her. Employees are given special treatment, such as stock options, profit sharing, Thanksgiving turkeys, year-end bonuses, and more.

Viking has added branches in nine European countries, Australia, and Japan. International operations produce over two-thirds of Viking's total revenues, with greater returns and profitability than most major competitors. These principles of "fanatical service" to their customers and employees, as well as highly advanced catalog marketing, had never been seen in Europe before

Viking introduced them. As a result, in recent years, growth and profitability have been even greater in Europe than in the United States. And before he recently retired, Irwin Helford happily reported that Viking had over 2 million loyal customers worldwide.

Effective advertising and PR will sell a product initially. But will a first-time buyer become a repeat buyer? That's the multi-million dollar question whose answer resides in customer service. Furnishing customers with better service than the good service they anticipated inspires buyer loyalty even more than price does. And buyer loyalty is infectious: your buyers actually all but sell your products for you. Whether you have a support staff or a one-person shop, take a page out of Irwin Helford's book and make the commitment of extraordinary service to your customers part of your business plan.

If you're going it alone, carrying out that commitment will be difficult, but worth the effort because it may be what distinguishes your enterprise from your competitors. By definition, your customers will be receiving owner-supplied personal service—something larger, more impersonal organizations unacquainted with Irwin Helford may not offer.

If you do have co-workers or employees, remember that because they help to carry out your plan, they must be eager to provide customers with the kind of service that will foster re-orders; and whether they have that attitude depends on the commitment their employer—your company—has made to them.

27

Your Greatest Assets

There once was an old Pakistani woman who worked as a water carrier for a rich man. She had two large pots that she carried on a pole. One of the pots was in perfect condition, the other had a crack in it.

Every day the water carrier went to the well, filled her pots, and carried them back to the master's house. However, along the way, water would leak out of the cracked pot so that by the time she reached her master's house it was only half-full.

This went on for many years until one day the cracked pot said to her miserably, "I'm so ashamed of myself. For years you have been carrying water in me and when we arrive at your master's house only half the water remains. You have only one-and-a-half pots of water, though you started out with two full pots. I'm just not very good at what I do."

The water carrier told the pot to cheer up and to look at the flowers on the side of the road the next time they went to the well.

The cracked pot did as she said and noticed that there were beautiful flowers all along the side of the road. He expressed his admiration to the water carrier, but said, "The flowers are beautiful, but they still don't make me feel better about being able only to deliver half a pot of water."

"But look at the other side of the road," said the water carrier. The cracked pot looked and saw that there were no flowers on that side. "You see," said the water carrier, "I took advantage of the water leaking out of you and planted seeds down your side of the road. Every day you have watered them, and I have been able to pick them and put fresh flowers on my master's table. If you had not been just the way you are, he would not have these beautiful flowers in his house."

Many of us are quick to see our shortcomings, yet we're often reluctant to recognize the importance of our strengths. I spend a great deal of my time paying attention to the morale and well-being of those whose strengths contribute to our company every day, our employees. They truly are our greatest assets, and I think of them not just as members of our company, but as people with families, needs, and dreams.

First, of course, we have to hire the right people. Here I learned some valuable things from Bob Adler, President of Bic while I was employed there. When Bob hired new managers, he always seemed to accord more weight to aggressiveness and instinct than academic credentials. In fact, he preferred hiring people like me who were unfamiliar with the industry so that he could help influence us. A new hire who has never worked in your specific industry is a clean slate you can imprint and mold with the company's values without interference from preconceptions. Bob followed up his hiring decisions with training that enhanced the employee's opportunity to succeed with the company.

Just as Bob did, I rely heavily on instincts in personnel matters. I personally interview and make the final decision to hire those executives in our company who report directly to me. After years of experience, I've noticed a few things. First, there are inevitably certain people who interview well but, once they start working, prove to be very different from the image they projected in their interviews. In order to keep this from happening to us, I used to be able to call as references people who previously supervised or employed the applicant. Now, however, in our highly litigious age, a court can hold one liable for giving a positive or a negative reference; so I find that personal references are suspect because many people are scared to give frank opinions. In fact, our attorneys have instructed us to give only specific dates of employment when we are called as references and not to offer any opinion about the former employee's performance—good or bad—in order to avoid a potential lawsuit.

So then, in the last analysis, I hire by instinct. As a salesman I had to be able to read people, and I think over the years I've proven to be a pretty good judge of character. An MBA has value, but I prefer to look for more important attributes like common sense, the way applicants handle themselves, and their attention spans (for example, during interviews, at what point does it seem like their minds start to wander?). Also, I always consider physical appearance. This might seem a little old-fashioned, but I've found that, especially for marketing people, there is a definite correlation between the way people look and their marketing ability. It's a simple matter of pride in appearance that translates into confidence.

The final "trick" I have learned to use over the years is, if the candidates make it to the third meeting, I will frequently ask them to bring their spouses along for a dinner interview. At first some people are surprised by this request. I am not interested in interviewing the spouse, but I've found that the spouse is a wonderful barometer of who the applicant is. I intuitively feel that choice of a life partner reflects a person's nature in a fundamental way. I am the first to admit that hiring still has a lot of mystery to it. I can do everything right and yet not have a person who fits into the company. But at least by employing these tools and rules, I feel that the majority of the people I hire are those who are best suited to working for us.

Hiring people is one thing; retaining them is quite another. I want Pilot to be a pleasant, safe, and happy place to work because when our employees thrive, the company prospers.

For this reason, we work a thirty-five hour week, either 7:30 to 3:30 or 8:30 to 4:30, with an hour off for lunch. Really! Instead of offering meditation rooms, foosball, or chair massages, I recognize that our employees have lives away from their jobs and should have the time and energy to live them. When they are at work, I want them to be comfortable. For example, when I was the number-two person at Pilot and we were building our Trumbull, Connecticut facility, I had the architect add air conditioning to the warehouse, even though the costs of installation and operation were daunting. I could not ask our employees to labor in a sweatbox during the summer while the rest of us worked in air-conditioned offices. But the air conditioning was not for their physical comfort alone; plainly, that environment would enhance their productivity as well.

When you treat your employees well, there is no limit to the contribution they can make to your company. Day after day it becomes more apparent that you cannot have tunnel vision about the roles employees have in your business. Many of them have valuable ideas they will share with you if you will only listen. After all, if it is made clear to them that they can't expect to succeed by seeking refuge in a job description, you have pretty much committed yourself to hear out their ideas. And we do. We have an employee suggestion box and any suggestion that we put into practice means an extra $100 for the person who offered the idea. Your business can't help but profit from such practices.

Because Mr. Tsuneto, Jack Paige, and many show business pros went out of their way to help me further my two careers, it's important to me to pass along that generosity. At Pilot Pen, we look first within our company for people to promote rather than immediately hire outside. We offer education reimbursement so our employees can advance their knowledge and skills. When employees are promoted, we delineate the scope and nature of their new responsibilities and what is expected of them, and otherwise work closely with them to help them succeed and do well.

Everybody wants to be a CEO, but the decisions you make once you are in a position of authority can have long-term ramifications that affect the lives of many people for years to come.

Much of life is a function of perspective and attitude. It's easy to get down on yourself and your company when things aren't going well, but it's more valuable to look around, regroup, and take definitive steps to make things work better. Let me illustrate this concept with a specific story about our sales force. For decades, we had relied on manufacturer's reps to sell our pens to all our outlets. The sales reps had done a great job for us, but I sensed it was time for a change. I knew we could do better with our own sales force.

So in 1988, when our sales reached $57 million, we decided to give up our sales reps. The reps were growing older and wealthier and were losing the energy and drive of earlier years. We figured we were getting about one-eighth of their selling time, and very few of the reps were willing to handle extra sales-building chores such as making personal consumer calls. In other words, it was time for a change.

Consequently, we decided to replace our one hundred reps with a forty-person in-house sales force to gain increased control over our sales effort. I have always believed that control is the key to managing one's future, and so we actively pursued taking back control.

However, this type of large transition always comes with many possible disastrous ramifications. We opted to move very carefully. We started not with an abrupt change, but a full six-month transitional period. We were also very concerned about the potential backlash from the sales reps. We didn't want the company to have to suffer any economic recriminations. In addition, we didn't want these people to feel they were being replaced because of their failures and, as a result, believe we were doing damage to their reputations. Our sales reps had been a major contributor to our growth and we wanted to make sure everybody knew that. And lastly, I was sensitive to the fact that angry ex-sales reps can do tremendous damage to a company's reputation. Simply put, we were extremely careful to avoid giving anyone a good reason to badmouth us, especially to our key accounts.

We implemented the transitional strategy accordingly:

1. We sent letters to all customers announcing the change, explaining the reasons for it, and emphasizing that Pilot Pen could improve its service under the new program.

2. We made sure this transition occurred across the whole country at the same time, thus minimizing any adverse effects on individual customers.

3. We devised severance packages to soften the economic blow to our reps. More specifically, in return for their agreement not to compete with Pilot for six months, we offered them full commission for the first month, gradually declining sums for the next four months, and then full commission again for the final month.

4. We divided the country into five sales regions, each with a field sales manager to oversee the new sales force. We authorized those sales managers to start recruiting the best sales candidates for each region. We developed selection criteria to evaluate the new recruits based upon our mission to not be the biggest but the best company in the pen business. Among other things, we sought people with substantial office-supply sales experience who were highly motivated self-starters, had a professional appearance and demeanor, and had a stable work history.

5. Recruiting was done by placing identical ads in local papers across the country. Of the hundreds of applicants, we chose at least ten in each region and subjected them to lengthy personal interviews and a battery of tests to evaluate them.

6. We developed company policy and training manuals for the new recruits. The regional sales managers then used those manuals as a guide during a week-long classroom training program that concentrated on product knowledge, company policies, reporting and operating procedures, and presentation skills. Then we had our field managers accompany our new recruits on all their customer calls the first week and on a diminishing proportion of calls during the next month.

7. To lure the high-caliber candidates our strategy demand-

ed, Pilot offered an attractive combination of salary, benefits, bonuses, and travel incentive contests offering trips to such locales as Monte Carlo and Japan.

When we completed our six-month transitional period, we finally had the control over our sales force that we always wanted. We could direct the sales team to focus on projects with longer-term, and potentially larger, payoffs. For example, one new task we implemented required the sales force to set aside at least one day a month to deliver new product samples. In addition, we also had them calling on smaller customers to promote the product, even though they don't in fact sell directly to such customers. Any orders resulting from these relationships would occur through our wholesalers, thus strengthening our relations with those dealers.

Two years after we had let our reps go, we had cut sales costs by $500,000 annually and sent sales revenues soaring, by close to 50 percent.

Recently, market conditions have changed so rapidly that we have needed to go back to sales reps in certain markets. Let me explain exactly how this has happened and why it is a good example of how one must constantly adjust to changing times.

We dropped our sales reps in 1988, coincidentally the year the big three office supply superstores—Office Depot, Staples, and Office Max—got started. To be honest, at first they were looked upon by the industry as a joke. We all thought that no one would want to walk into a huge "warehouse" store to buy office supplies.

How Wrong Could We Have Been?

We had no idea of the great impact these superstores would have on the sale of office products. In a matter of a few years, the big three ended up putting 8,000 small office supply stores out of business. As we rolled through the nineties, the small mom-and-pop stationery stores couldn't compete with the superstores' prices.

With the loss of the mom-and-pop stores, we also found that

fewer direct salespeople were needed. Currently, we have one salesman who works only with the big three customers. He is forever traveling between the Delray Beach headquarters of Office Depot in Florida, greater Boston to meet with Staples, and the Office Max people in greater Cleveland.

Today, we have a combination: We use some direct in-house salespeople, and we have reemployed several manufacturers' representatives. The direct salespeople we have serve an important function, and we plan to keep them, but it has become clear that we also need sales reps.

Hiring and promoting employees and structuring the sales force are functions I enjoy. Firing people, on the other hand, is the hardest thing I have to do. One specific incident comes to mind from my days as national sales manager at Bic. This is a hard-to-believe but true story. One of Bic's own salespeople was sending anti-Semitic letters to the company with his signature on them. Bob Adler, the president and CEO, happened to be Jewish and was very disturbed by these letters. It's bad enough to receive anonymous anti-Semitic threats from the public, let alone signed notes from an employee.

Bob called me into his office and we devised a strategy. Bob believed that as sales manager, I should act on this matter but not act too rashly or harshly. I felt this employee could be reformed, so I took charge and spent time meeting with him, trying to tell him that this kind of activity was simply unacceptable. I went out of my way to do everything possible to squelch his intolerance, but the letters kept coming nonetheless.

Finally, after weeks of meeting with this salesman, I felt we had no recourse and couldn't afford to wait any longer; this guy's employment had to be terminated. Upon being informed of his firing, our disgruntled salesman took off in his company car. Now, technically, this act made his car stolen property. He had to give the car back to us, and turn in his samples, which were still in the vehicle. Fortunately, he drove straight to his house, where the police were able to find him and get our property back.

We thought that was the end of the matter, but the following Sunday morning our former salesman went to church with his family. During the service, he excused himself to go to the men's room. Instead of going to the men's room, however, he walked behind the church and put a bullet through his head.

It was naturally very difficult for his family and friends to deal with his suicide. For a long time I wondered if I could have handled his situation differently and thereby helped avert this tragedy. In the end, I've come to realize that we had no alternative and acted appropriately. If he had stayed at the company any longer as his mental health deteriorated, he might have harmed employees or even members of his family.

While telling someone that he or she is no longer employed is the worst part of being a boss, this incident has caused me to bring even more sensitivity to these meetings. For example, when I or one of our managers has to let someone go, we tell that person on a Monday or Tuesday. This gives the person the balance of the week to start looking for a new job and some feeling of control over his or her work life. We never fire employees on a Friday, because we don't want them anguishing over their misfortune over the weekend.

In all but a few states, there is no such thing as firing at will anymore. Any job termination must be accompanied by a long paper trail documenting all the employee's work deficiencies that led to his or her termination. In my experience, when I recognize someone needs to go, I usually give the employee another chance, and invariably, I am stung by this inclination. So, no matter how hard I try to safeguard their jobs, soon enough I have to let them go anyway.

Advancement in your company to the executive level of management generally means you will assume some personnel decisions and recommendations. Experience has taught me that in discharging those responsibilities, several important principles are worthwhile implementing.

In hiring, rely on your instincts to determine whether a person will be a good fit with your company.

When you treat your employees well, they will tend to develop a proprietary attitude about your business that will reward your company.

Giving promotion priority to existing employees helps build morale, and as a consequence, strengthens your company.

Adapt and change the structure of your sales force to fit changes in your markets; but whether your salespeople are in-house or outside, treat them well. (Are you getting the message regarding the treatment of people who work for you?)

Since I was abruptly fired at Bic, I have had a sensitivity to the havoc an unforeseen termination can inflict on an individual and his or her family, emotionally as well as financially. Accordingly, if a job termination must take place, it must be done in the most sensitive and humane way possible.

28

When Saving Money Is a Lousy Investment

When I was visiting a new account one day, I heard this story about an elderly couple in Kansas, Stumpy and Esther. Stumpy got his nickname because he was built like a fireplug. He was a sweet, quiet man who was constantly henpecked by his wife, Esther. Every year, they'd go to the Kansas State Fair, and every year Stumpy would say, "Esther, I'd like to ride in that there airplane."

And every year Esther would say, "I know, Stumpy, but that airplane ride costs ten dollars, and ten dollars is ten dollars."

One year, Stumpy and Esther went to the fair and Stumpy said, "Esther, I'm eighty-one years old. If I don't ride that airplane this year, I may never get another chance."

Esther replied, "Stumpy, that there airplane ride costs ten dollars, and ten dollars is ten dollars."

The pilot overheard them and said, "Folks, look. For years I've been hearing you argue, so let me make you a deal. I'll take you both up for a ride. If you can stay quiet for the entire ride and not say a word, I promise I won't charge you, but if you say even one word, it's gonna cost you ten dollars!"

Stumpy and Esther agreed and up they went. The pilot did all kinds of twists and turns, rolls and dives, but not a word was spoken by either of them.

So then, he did all his tricks over again, but still, neither Stumpy nor Esther uttered a word.

When they landed, the pilot turned to Stumpy, "By golly, I did everything I could think of to get you to yell out, but you didn't even say one word, so I guess your ride'll be free."

Stumpy replied, "Well, I was gonna say something when Esther fell out, but ten dollars is ten dollars."

As a CEO, I know how important it is to contain costs, but I'm also the first to remind my fellow board members that you have to spend money to make money. The vision of a company must be broad-based and longsighted. You can't get so absorbed in saving ten dollars that you lose sight of your employees, customers, and the millions of other dollars that could be coming in.

To illustrate this point, I love to tell the story of Thomas G. Stemberg, a true business visionary. Fresh out of Harvard Business School, Tom joined Jewel's Star Market's corporate training program in 1973. He rose to vice president of sales and merchandising by 1980. He moved to Connecticut-based First National Supermarkets, where he held various senior management positions and was promoted to president of the company's Edwards-Finast division. At Edwards-Finast, he devised a revolutionary plan of cost-cutting warehouse stores, buying in volume and slashing prices. After working so hard, Tom asked to be rewarded appropriately. The company's response was to let him go.

On the Friday afternoon of a Fourth of July weekend a short while after he was fired, Tom was working at home in West Hartford, Connecticut, when his printer ribbon ran out. He went to a series of stationery stores in search of a replacement ribbon, only to find that none was open. When he finally found a wholesale club store that was open, it didn't carry the ribbon he needed. Unable to print without a ribbon, Tom saw an opportunity in his predicament. He believed there was an untapped market of frustrated consumers and small business owners who couldn't easily find the office supplies they needed and, when they could, were overpaying because they couldn't buy in volume. Tom envisioned millions of them patronizing an office products superstore stocked with thousands of items at discount prices.

To test his theory, he called a very large paper products company and tried to order a direct shipment of paper for what he claimed was a small company of twenty employees. The best deal the company would give him was a 20 percent discount. Shortly thereafter, he called back, claiming he was with a large company of over one hundred employees, and this time he got more than a 50 percent discount. Tom was thrilled. His instincts were right. The average consumer and small business owner were not able to get the discounts they wanted and deserved. It was at that moment that Tom became certain he was onto something big and quickly moved forward on his office supply superstore concept.

To turn his concept into reality, Tom got together with a retired former competitor he greatly respected from the supermarket industry who wanted to get back into business and had access to capital. Together, they put together a business plan and management team. After a few months of long days and nights, the first Staples store opened its doors in Massachusetts in 1986. By developing Staples into a retail outlet designed to slash the cost and eliminate the hassle of purchasing office supplies, Tom created a company that now does $7 billion a year in business. Under his leadership, Staples became one of only six companies to ever reach $5 billion in sales within ten years.

Tom's success resulted from his objective to meet the increasingly sophisticated needs of small business customers by providing low-cost products and fast, efficient, convenient service while creating growth vehicles for the future. Tom has propelled Staples to 33 percent earnings per share compounded annual growth over the last five years. This growth has been fueled by an aggressive store expansion program, a profitable office products delivery business, a growing international presence, the recently launched e-commerce site Staples.com, and strategic acquisitions such as mail order marketer Quill Corporation.

* * *

Clearly, Tom is a brilliant businessman, and First National would have been well served by rewarding his service to their company instead of firing him. But Tom believes if he hadn't been fired, he might still be with First National today and Staples would have never been born.

Shortsighted people find only frustration when normal sources lack something they require. Others, like Tom, have the open-mindedness to see that deficiencies represent needs to be satisfied. In simple terms, supplying the products and services to fill those needs is the business of business. Beyond this, it takes clear vision and entrepreneurial spirit to profitably satisfy a "new" need with a new venture. While not everyone is willing to take the risks associated with establishing a new enterprise, there is everything to be gained by at least identifying the deficiencies which could ripen into unserved and underserved markets. How else do you think business expands?

29

Creating New Markets

B esides being home to Pilot Pen of America, greater New Haven is also the original home of Lender's Bagel Bakery. For many years, I've been fortunate to be friends, and work closely on several charitable and community committees, with the brains behind Lender's Bagels, Murray and Marvin Lender. Their success story is a prime example of two individuals having extraordinary foresight and the passion to act upon their vision.

In the 1930s and 1940s, Murray and Marvin Lender's parents literally had a backyard business baking bagels in the garage behind their small house. From this inauspicious beginning, baking an ethnic specialty food generally consumed mainly on Sunday mornings by Jewish people, evolved into a huge business where billions of bagels are consumed every year by all kinds of people worldwide.

Things really started to change in 1955 when Murray and Marvin first put their bagels into polyethylene bags and took their product to supermarkets around New England. Because the bagels still had a short shelf life, however, further innovations were necessary if sales were to grow. In 1962, two dramatic advances occurred. First, the Lenders worked with a company to produce the first automated bagel-baking machine. Now, instead of having to train bakers for six months on the specialized techniques of making bagels, machines working twenty-four hours a day could produce hundreds of thousands of bagels a month.

Second, the Lenders started freezing sliced bagels, thus locking in their freshness and providing their product with a practically unlimited shelf life. This was probably the single most important innovation in allowing Lender's Bagels to go beyond the local area and to have a national presence. The Lenders chose to use a sales force of frozen food brokers (120 different brokerage firms), who pushed for years until they succeeded in getting Lender's frozen bagels into virtually every frozen food aisle in North America. Meanwhile, as the brokers pushed to help them penetrate the country's markets, the Lenders built the first automated bagel-baking plant.

By 1977, Lender's Bagels had reached nationwide distribution, and they started spending more money on advertising and sales incentives for their brokers. By 1984, Lender's was grossing $60 million a year and, that year, was sold to Kraft Foods for $90 million. At the time of the Kraft purchase, Lender's Bagels was employing 600 people and had three plants in the United States. As a consequence, the Lenders felt they could no longer keep personally attuned to their day-to-day operations. Murray and Marvin were working fifteen hours a day, seven days a week. What started out as a family business was losing that personalized, family touch. Meanwhile, they had already been doing some co-promotion deals with Kraft Foods, which at that time had no frozen food products. The buyout seemed a marriage made in heaven.

But there was a problem. The Lenders feared that after the buyout their brokers might lose faith in their product. To reassure their brokers, the Lenders came up with a brilliant idea. At the national sales meeting, they staged a huge fancy wedding ceremony that included dinner, drinks, and dancing. The Lenders called it the Wedding of the Century, and they had actors dressed in costumes designed to look like the major Kraft and Lender's products. A two-legged bag of Lender's Bagels and huge canister of Philadelphia Cream Cheese walked down the aisle just as in a wedding. Then they exchanged vows and were betrothed. The brokers cheered and cried and ate and drank and everybody had a great time.

Murray and Marvin stayed on with Kraft for a few years to ease the company's transition, and by 1992, 1.5 billion Lender's Bagels were sold a year. Every person who owns a corner bagel store today owes a small debt to the Lender brothers for making the bagel not just another ethnic treat, but part of American culture.

After Murray had stopped working at the company, he was still acting as its TV spokesperson. One day I invited him to have lunch so that I could convince him to allow us to honor him with a dinner for his work with the Anti-Defamation League. Murray has always been a great philanthropist, and I thought to have a dinner honoring him would be the natural thing to do. However, he came to that lunch with his own agenda. He wanted to try to convince me to appear in TV commercials for Pilot pens. Murray believed that the success Lender's had with him doing their commercials could be equaled by the success Pilot could have with me in our commercials. Murray felt that my personality would lend itself to commercials, and he pressed me to do them. He argued that in many ways my entire life experiences in performing and sales were perfect training for me to do television commercials.

This wasn't the first time that someone I respected lobbied me to appear in our TV ads. For years, Don Aaronson and Stan Pearlman from our ad agency had also tried to persuade me to step in front of the camera. Looking back at that lunch, I think we both succeeded that day. I was able to get Murray to agree to be the honoree for our fund-raising dinner, and I began appearing in our TV commercials.

The Lenders are a truly great American business success story. And it all really started with the Lenders' ability to stand back and see the market potential of a product that others ignored. So, whether you are selling Dr. Grip pens, frozen bagels, or any other product, your marketing mandate is to have a vision that extends beyond the ordinary. And if that vision is clear and true, you will reap huge financial benefits for the rest of your life.

30

Failure Is a Great Teacher

There were once two very successful businessmen who were brothers. They attended church regularly, pretending to be good, honest Christians. The truth was, however, they were evil to the core. They were extremely rich but hoarded their money and then put it to ill use.

One day the pastor of the church retired and a new one was appointed. He soon saw right through these two brothers but kept quiet. He was an inspiring pastor, and the church membership grew and grew. He even started a fundraising campaign to fix the church roof.

Then one of the brothers died suddenly in a car accident. Before the funeral, the other brother handed the pastor a check for the full amount needed to fix the roof. He said to the pastor, "You can have this on one condition. At the funeral you must say that my brother was a saint."

The pastor promised to do so and cashed the check.

The next day, at the funeral, the pastor stood up and told the truth but kept his word, saying, "He was an evil man. He cheated on his wife, abused his family, and was cruel to others. But compared to his brother— he was a saint."

It's easy to pull the wool over people's eyes. It's easy to lie and to paint a more saintly picture of yourself, especially when you have a public relations machine behind you, as many companies do today.

But always be careful; one day, the truth may be exposed. Remember what James E. Burke, former chairman and CEO of

Johnson & Johnson, did when the Extra-Strength Tylenol poison scare struck the country in 1982 (Tylenol is a product of Johnson & Johnson's McNeil Consumer Products Company). He did not try to evade responsibility. He did not try to hide. He immediately took full responsibility and recalled the product nationwide. Johnson & Johnson suffered short-term financial losses, but as a result of his actions, people never lost faith in the product, and Tylenol soon was selling better than ever. Deception will catch up to you, but truth and acceptance of responsibility will build consumer confidence.

So far, I've related a series of business success stories, but I would be presenting a false picture of myself and Pilot Pen Corporation of America if I didn't also share with you a few stories of some of the products with which we've been associated that have really BOMBED!

My favorite failure anecdote has to be the tale of the Pilot Brougham pen. Never heard of the Pilot Brougham? Well, there's a very good reason for that—the Brougham came and went really fast. Let me tell you exactly what happened.

In North America, Pilot has always been known for fine-point or extra-fine-point pens. In fact, we are the only large manufacturer of ballpoint pens that sells more fine-point than medium-point pens. And even though the fine point put us on the map, we still wanted to get a larger share of the medium-point market. So, we decided to go in the opposite direction and make a broad-point pen. In other words, the average medium-point pen has a 0.7 millimeter ball, but we opted to go with a larger, 1.0 millimeter ball. We were excited about the possibilities, especially since the larger ball allows for a smoother line.

So we jumped into manufacturing this new broad-point pen. The new pen was going to be my baby, and I really wanted to make it a classy-looking writing instrument. We chose a beautiful charcoal gray color for the pen body and a shiny silver clip on the cap.

We designed it in-house with a little help from a design company. I knew it had to have an imposing name. We played with lots of titles, but none seemed to click. I was driving an Oldsmobile Regency Brougham at the time, so I thought—what a perfect name for a pen, the Regency. But this name was already taken. So, we settled for the name, *Brougham*, which means a high-class carriage. In fact, it was a name used by Cadillac. So, there it was. Our new broad-point pen—the new Pilot Brougham. I thought it couldn't miss.

Unfortunately, we laid a horrible egg and lost millions. The Brougham didn't write as smoothly as it was supposed to. The name *Brougham* was hard to pronounce and hard for most Americans to remember. After a year, when we knew we had a real flop on our hands, we sold our inventory at cost and took the loss. It was my fault. It was my pet project, and there was nobody else I could blame for its failure. So, I stood naked in the spotlight and took the blame.

A few years later, we invested in a great office product that we were sure would be a huge seller. It was called the Grippa—in honor of the way it really gripped paper! The Grippa was a plastic paper holder that attached to the side of any desktop computer monitor to hold a piece of paper at eye level, thus making it much easier for people working at a keyboard to enter information. I fell in love with this product when I saw how cleverly it was bent and curved to beautifully hold a piece of paper without ever allowing it to fold over.

The Grippa was designed by a man in England. We made a deal for the rights to sell the Grippa in North America at a retail price of $17.95. In this case our parent company in Japan was not involved. Again, this was my baby. When we first demonstrated the Grippa to our wholesalers, they flipped over it. They all said they'd never seen anything like it. Since we were receiving such great support from them, we eagerly moved forward. We designed a special Grippa box and packaged it beautifully. Unbeknownst to us and our wholesalers, however, at this time a similar product designed to hold paper was about to be released by one of our competitors at a price of $10.99. As soon as we learned this fact, we realized we were virtually dead in the water at the outset. Again, we took a big financial hit.

In both of these cases, I was saddened by our inability to make the Grippa and the Brougham into viable business success-es, but I didn't allow our company to dwell on our losses. Instead, we focused on our growing sales of other products and learned whatever we could from our mistakes.

The business road just isn't a smooth superhighway marked with successive milestones of success. Your mother was right: everyone, but everyone makes mistakes. When you make yours, admit it; don't gloss over it. Then objectively appraise where you went wrong and what, if anything, you could have done to avoid your error. And specifically, if you ever find yourself backing a product or idea that can't take off, get out quickly and move on.

31

Overcome Setbacks with Tenacity

T hough I play golf, my passion is tennis, especially since Pilot Pen has been involved in one of the top women's tennis tournaments in the country. But I'm getting ahead of myself. Here's a suspenseful tale of a business situation that could have become a catastrophe but ended up a victory.

It was a winter day in 1982. I was getting a haircut at Vinny's Barber Shop in New Haven. As Vinny did his magic, Larry Hoffman walked in. Larry was an active member of the local Probus Club, a charitable organization whose main goal is to raise funds for handicapped and autistic children. Larry told me that the club had been approved to do a little Challenger Series tennis event in New Haven, but they had limited funds and needed to find a title sponsor.

The previous year, Bic Pen had sponsored the event, which took place in August at Southern Connecticut State University. Bic decided not to renew its sponsorship, however, throwing the Probus Club's tournament and primary fund-raiser in jeopardy. Right there in the barbershop, Larry offered Pilot the chance to take over the title sponsorship. I expected it would cost around $75,000, but like any good businessperson in a negotiation, I kept a "poker face" and asked, "Larry, how much?"

He looked at me and said, "It's only going to cost you five thousand dollars."

I wasn't sure if I heard him right and asked, "Larry, excuse me, but would you repeat that?"

"Just five thousand bucks."

"Okay," I said, "we might be able to do that. But the name of the tournament has to be only three words long and two of the words have to be Pilot Pen."

Larry agreed, we shook hands, and the Pilot Pen Open was born in the barbershop. The first day of the tournament, only twelve people showed up, and I was a friend to eleven of them. I panicked. What a horrible waste of money! I was mortified. I went home depressed and embarrassed. However, as I was reading the paper the next morning, I noticed how many times Pilot was mentioned and realized, "Hey, wait a second! Maybe our little tournament wasn't such a failure after all."

The truth was, we received a tremendous amount of favorable publicity for sponsoring the tournament, much more than we could have received spending $5,000 on ordinary advertising. We continued to sponsor the event each August, and in 1984, during the third Pilot Pen Open, an idea began fidgeting in my imagination. What would happen if we became the title sponsor of a *major* tournament with really big name players? I studied the demographics of people who play tennis recreationally and saw a huge correlation with Pilot pen users. I contacted our ad agency, which made an introduction to a sports management company. Our timing was perfect. The title sponsor of a major tennis tournament wanted out, and the tournament director was talking with potential sponsors.

Within two weeks of hatching this idea, I met with the tournament director, Charlie Pasarell, at the U.S. Open in nearby Flushing, New York. Charlie made his presentation, and I liked what I heard. He also said one of the major automotive companies was very interested in taking over the title sponsorship. I knew that big corporations meant many layers of approval, and I had a window of opportunity. I asked Charlie whether, if I made a decision on the spot, we'd have a deal. Charlie said we would. That's how, in addition to sponsoring the little Pilot Pen Open, we became the sponsor of the Pilot Pen Classic, held each February in Palm Springs, California.

For the next three years, from 1985 through 1987, Pilot Pen received a great deal of positive publicity across the country. Before it was time to renew our option to continue sponsoring the classic, I learned that the tournament organizers were trying to raise more money from another sponsor. We quickly renewed our contract to lock us in for the next three years at the same fee we had been paying. The organizers of the event were now in a bind. They were contractually obligated to work with us, but they had interest from a larger corporation with more financial clout. In the end, we worked out a deal that we felt was very fair and economically advantageous to us. We decided to withdraw as title sponsor of the classic.

Meanwhile, the Pilot Pen Open in New Haven kept going, finally ending in 1991 after a ten-year run. At the same time, the Volvo International Tennis Tournament, a major Association of Tennis Professionals (ATP) men's event, moved to New Haven in 1990 and was doing well. In 1994, however, Volvo notified the owner of the tournament that it was no longer interested in being title sponsor, and the owner had two years to find a replacement. The tournament owner talked to many companies that were bigger than Pilot and came up empty. Finally, he came to see me. I gave him a price. He laughed at our offer and was not interested. For the next two years, he kept talking to other companies, but unsuccessfully. Finally, he became so desperate that he returned to us and agreed to the original price he'd laughed at two years earlier. In 1996, we became the title sponsor of the newly named Pilot Pen International.

We were thrilled to be involved with another large, prestigious tournament that featured the top men's players in the world at one of the country's finest facilities. A few years earlier, the state of Connecticut had built a 15,000-seat, $18 million-facility on the grounds of Yale University, in New Haven. At the time, it was the second largest outdoor tennis stadium in the United States. Only the Stadium Court at the USTA National Tennis Center in Flushing, home of the U.S. Open, was bigger. Since the tournament is held in late August—the week before the U.S. Open—we looked forward to crowds of fans, ideal weather, and considerable media coverage. We envisioned the Pilot Pen International as a natural lead-in for the U.S. Open. Because of the timing and since Connecticut is one of the most affluent states in the country, our tournament's potential seemed unlimited. In fact, the purse had been raised from $675,000 to $1,040,000 to take advantage of the combination of the money, the market, the stadium, and the time of year. In doing so, the hope was that Connecticut would grow to have an irresistible draw as host to the pre-U.S. Open tournament.

But our euphoria was quickly deflated. Within five months of becoming the title sponsor, we faced a crisis. In January 1997, we discovered that the tournament owner was in serious financial trouble, and it was very possible there would not be a tournament that summer. The 1996 tournament had a terribly disappointing attendance. The crowds weren't coming because many of the high-profile players chose the ATP tournament in Indianapolis, which was played that same week, instead of coming to New Haven. The tournament owner was in debt somewhere between $2 and $4 million.

Linda Lorimer, Yale University vice president responsible for relations with the city of New Haven, met with the owner in January. He opened his books to Yale, revealing that the money brought in for the upcoming tournament had already been spent. He suggested that an investor be found. Immediately after their meeting, Linda called me to express her alarm. I was aware of the tournament's recent history of dwindling attendance and the diminished promotion for the upcoming event, so her call came as no surprise. The loss of the tournament would be a huge black eye for Yale, New Haven, and of course Pilot. No one wanted to lose this event. Serious action had to be taken, and quickly.

I was motivated by visions of angry ticket holders protesting outside our headquarters and demanding refunds—and the media picking up the story that would discredit Pilot across the country. Even though we were just the title sponsor and had nothing to do with administration of the tournament, it was our name that was associated with the event, and thus it was our corporate reputation that was on the line. Yale and New Haven held large stakes in this tournament's success, as well. Although Yale is one of the top universities, it competes for students. Parents consider the totality of a university's offerings and this high-level tournament enhanced Yale's appeal. The city of New Haven recognized the tourism and economic benefits from the tournament, as well as the prestige of being the host city. Compounding the problems of losing the tournament was the chance the press would discover the fiscal crisis. With such juicy bait as Yale, Pilot, and the city of New Haven, if reporters uncovered this story, it would be like blood in the water.

Linda discretely arranged a private meeting among Yale president Rick Levin, the mayor of New Haven, herself, and me. After much discussion, we agreed we had to immediately search for a way to bring in someone new. Rick and Linda said they'd search among Yale graduates for tennis promoters and tournament directors. I agreed to meet with the owner to assess the situation.

The owner and I met. Because of his monetary distress, the 1997 tournament itself and its promotion were being severely cut back. At the next Yale-New Haven-Pilot meeting, I reported the worsening news. Linda and Rick produced their list of candidates to rescue the tournament. They asked if I had a list. I gave them a piece of paper with one name written five times: Butch Buchholz.

Butch was a top tennis player in the 1960s, touring and competing with champions such as Jack Kramer, Frank Sedgman, Pancho Gonzalez, and Pancho Segura. Butch competed until injuries forced him to retire in 1970. But he didn't leave tennis. He went on to become one of the country's most successful tournament promoters and owners, including founding the Lipton

Championships in 1985 (now named the Nasdaq-100).

Over the years I had watched Butch's tournament in Key Biscayne, Florida grow into one of the world's top tennis events. It was well run and brilliantly promoted, consistently attracted the world's top men's and women's players, and brought in sellout crowds. In fact, box seats to the Lipton were so hard to come by they were bequeathed in wills. I absolutely believed that bringing in Butch was our only shot at salvaging the Pilot Pen International and turning it into a successful event. Rick, Linda, and the mayor agreed that Butch was our strongest option, and since I had met him once at a cocktail party, I was elected to contact him at his office in Miami.

I called. Butch was aware that our tournament was in trouble. The current owner had already contacted him about becoming his partner and infusing the event with new cash. However, Butch had no interest in becoming a partner; he needed to be in charge. I talked with him about the problems we faced, but also pointed out the potential, particularly since our tournament was the week before the U.S. Open. I confessed my concerns about ticket holders losing their money and Pilot's reputation being damaged. Butch said he'd come to New Haven to meet with the owner and look at the numbers.

He did, and he still wasn't interested in a partnership. But I hadn't lost interest in Butch. He agreed to meet me in Miami so we could talk face-to-face. When I arrived, I was shocked to see that the Pilot Pen tournament owner was there for the meeting! Naturally, his presence inhibited what I could discuss. After I returned home, I phoned Butch and told him what I had wanted to say in person. Pilot, Yale, and New Haven would agree to bring him in as the sole owner, not as a partner. Butch was intrigued but pragmatic. In addition to the Lipton, he was creating a new tournament in Latin America. He didn't need the business and his family was unwilling to lose even more of his time.

After eleven years of reading audiences and three decades of reading customers, I sensed that Butch was attracted to the challenge and that his only reluctance was displeasing his family. I persevered in my campaign until Butch said he'd meet with his family to discuss his taking over our tournament. A few days later, Butch phoned and with great enthusiasm said he'd take us on. He'd buy out the tournament owner, accept the debt that had been incurred, put his own money into our event, and run it as a top tennis tournament. I was thrilled! I called Rick and Linda at Yale and the mayor with the good news. We rejoiced that the tournament had been saved and the story had been kept out of the papers.

However, this bout of euphoria was also short-lived. Butch called me five days later to say his involvement was off. He just couldn't take on one more project. He told me that this was a very tough call for him. Since it was the end of February and our tournament was less than six months away, the call was even tougher for me. I pleaded with Butch to reconsider, and probed for any new reasons for his sudden turnabout. Butch brought up an obstacle that he felt was the deal breaker. He initially thought he could get around it but realized he could not. I assured him we could take care of it, and again asked him to reconsider. He agreed to let me know in a week. Six days later, he called to say we were on again.

It was now March. Phissy and I were in Washington, D.C. to attend a fundraiser at the Kennedy Center. While we were dressing in our hotel room, the phone rang. Butch had tracked me down. My stomach clenched and my heart sank as I heard him say, "Ron, this is the most difficult phone call of my life. It's final. I can't do it." By the end of the call we were late for our event so we hurried to the Kennedy Center. I was so distraught that Phissy and I went to the wrong cocktail reception, nibbling someone else's refreshments for half an hour before we figured out why we didn't recognize anyone. We ducked out and I found a pay phone to call the mayor with the bad news. He agreed to set up an early morning meeting in New Haven the next day with Rick, Linda, himself, and me.

The four of us knew we had to find a solution in record time. We discussed who else we could approach. However, I remained convinced that Butch was our man and that he really wanted to take a swipe at this challenge. I felt confident that if I could sit with him face-to-face one more time, I could sell him. I suggested that we ask Butch if he would accept a meeting with the four of us. I thought that if he accepted, we were halfway there. The others agreed and began consulting their schedules. I interrupted to say that we had to go *today*. Every hour that passed worked against us. There were protests about the impossibility of getting a flight to Miami that day, but I would not accept impossibility. If Butch said he would meet us, I said we'd charter a plane. The expense would be negligible compared to the cost of losing the tournament.

Since it was still early in the morning, I called Butch at home. He said he would meet with us and that he'd pick us up at the airport. I told him we could get there by 3:00. We chartered a small jet and landed at five minutes before 3:00. (Rick Levin was the only one who could not make the trip, since he was meeting several world dignitaries at Yale that day.) Butch had just arrived at the airport as well. Since the Lipton was opening in a few days, he drove us to the stadium and gave us a tour before we sat down for an early dinner. We didn't have much time. Our jet had to be back in the air before 9:00 for our pilots to fly legally.

Once our meals were served, it was my time to be on. I never sold so hard in my life. I pitched my heart out to Butch. Linda and the mayor stepped in to add information and answer questions. Butch brought up his list of concerns. One by one, the mayor and Linda said that each would be addressed. Anything that Butch needed, they said they'd handle. The three of us came up with ways for him to get everything he wanted. It was close to 8:30, and the sky was thick with rain clouds; lightning and thunder bolted through the heavy air. Butch rushed us back to the airport. At ten minutes before 9:00, Butch and I stood in the rain beside the jet, facing each other. I asked when I should call him. He said that he'd call me the next day, one way or the other. We shook hands, I boarded, and we took off.

The next morning I told Patty Skarupa, my assistant, that when Butch Buchholz called she should track me down no matter where I might be in the building. Though I had plenty to do, the day dragged by. Even though I believed that Butch wanted to take over the tournament, we'd gone back and forth so many times that I didn't know what his final decision would be. I was deeply concerned about what we would do if Butch said no. Finally, at 3:15, Butch called. The deal was on!

With less than five months before the tournament's opening day, Butch officially agreed to take the reins. The Pilot Pen International was saved! Needless to say, we were ecstatic. Butch was our white knight who galloped in at the last minute.

In the first two years, he lost $2.2 million, but he stayed with it. In 1999, for the first time, the event turned a profit. Furthermore, Mike Davies, a former tennis star from the U.K., moved to New Haven and became president of the tournament. Working with him is tournament director Anne Worcester, who previously served as CEO of the Women's Tennis Association (WTA). Butch continues as the chairman of the event.

Today, the tournament is called Pilot Pen Tennis and features professional women exclusively, attracting the top players in the world. It has grown into the tournament we envisioned and continues to get even better. And we've adhered to the requirement I gave Larry Hoffman in Vinny's Barber Shop on that long-ago winter day—the name is three words long, with two of them being Pilot Pen.

Getting involved in a small, basically unknown tennis tournament in 1982 has led to many significant dividends for us to this day. Our sponsorship of the tournament, through publicity generated by television and newspaper coverage of the event, the name

Pilot Pen reached infinitely more potential customers than our advertising budgets possibly could have targeted. It also reinforced three valuable lessons:

1. Develop a vision for any major endeavor.
2. Identify and recruit the best talent.
3. Hold on to that vision with tenacity.

I also learned a lesson that may have helped save someone's life.

32

Impossibility Is Not an Option

H oward and Sandie Taubin have been very close friends to Phissy and me for years. Howard is a doctor, a gastroenterologist, and Sandie works in a law firm. Every year they attend the Pilot Pen Tennis tournament. One year, following the day's matches, they drove to Cape May Courthouse in New Jersey, about 225 miles away, a solid five-hour drive with traffic.

Not long after they arrived at their destination, Howard complained he wasn't feeling well. He developed a fever, chills, and severe muscle aches. Six hours later, he was transported to the local hospital by ambulance. His condition deteriorated so quickly that he was lapsing in and out of consciousness.

After an examination and a few blood tests, he was given a diagnosis of flu. However, Howard's condition worsened. His coloring turned gray, and his vital signs became unstable. Sandie grew frantic and called Howard's medical partner, Dr. Greg Soloway, in Stratford, Connecticut, relaying the symptoms. Dr. Soloway said to have Howard tested for meningitis and demanded that he be started on the appropriate medication.

Sure enough, meningitis was the correct diagnosis, and Howard had contracted the deadly meningococcal meningitis. Sandie telephoned us at home and we knew from the fright in her voice that it was serious. We dropped everything, rushed to the car, defied speed limits, and arrived at the hospital within five hours of Sandie's call.

It was worse than we feared. Howard was in the intensive care unit in isolation and could have only one visitor at a time. I suited up in that blue sterile hospital garb and was heartsick to hear Howard quietly say, "Ronnie, I think this is the big one." His doctors seemed to agree.

It made me nuts to know that if this had happened while Howard was at home, he'd be cared for like royalty in his own hospital in Bridgeport and have a better chance at pulling through. I plunged into finding a way to get him medically evacuated in an airplane. While transporting him in his condition was extremely risky, he didn't seem to have any options if he stayed where he was. Sandie was understandably distraught. I couldn't ask her to make a decision that might save her husband or kill him.

We tracked down Howard's brother Joel, also a doctor, but he was traveling and couldn't get to Cape May Courthouse until the next morning. Howard hung on while we waited. I had a medical evacuation team on standby. Finally Joel arrived and examined Howard. Joel told me that his brother had a fifty-fifty chance of surviving a flight home. I persuaded him to go for it and we put Operation Howard in motion.

A medical evacuation plane comes with a pilot, co-pilot, and nurse. Joel accompanied Howard on the flight to Connecticut, which was met by ambulance at the Bridgeport airport. Howard was rushed to the hospital, where a medical A-team of his colleagues was waiting to meet him. In the meantime, Phissy, Sandie, and I drove home, checking on Howard's progress by phone and struggling to prevent fear from overtaking us.

Howard survived the medical evacuation and spent weeks in the hospital recovering. Today he is healthy, fit, and practicing medicine again. He credits me and many others with saving his life. I believe a higher power is responsible for getting him through that flight; however, I am deeply grateful that I was able to be there for my friend.

* * *

Experiences like this are kicks in the head for remembering what is truly important. I also relearned the value of creating options when there appear to be none, and to summon the courage to push forward and make things happen when the result would be worth the risk.

33

Profit Isn't Everything

One Broadway theater tried to save money in a unique way. Instead of installing a rising orchestra pit, the producers had the orchestra just stand up slowly!

E ver since I was a youngster, standing on stage in a big glowing white spotlight, I've always dreamed that someday I would open my own theater.

In the late 1980s, as passing thoughts of retirement started to creep into my head, in an effort to find out if I really would like being in the theater administration business, I got involved with the legendary Shubert Theater in downtown New Haven, Connecticut.

It all started out rather innocently. I was tapped to chair a big fundraiser for the New Haven Jewish Home for the Aged. Not sure what we would do for the fundraiser, I decided, as Mickey Rooney and Judy Garland would have, that we should put on a show. First, we booked a big-name performer, and to really make it an exceptional event, I insisted that we do it at a special venue, someplace with cachet, with history. There's no place in Connecticut with more ties to the legends of Broadway than the Shubert Theater, frequently a "tryout" stop for new shows headed for Broadway.

We arranged to get Neil Sedaka to headline. After he was booked, my close friend ever since my Miami days, the talented Rosemary Clooney, gave me a call and said she was going to be in

Massachusetts around the time of the fundraiser. On her way back to New York, she agreed to stop by and sing a few songs—for no pay, mind you—just to help. I opened with a few minutes of my shtick, and then I introduced Rosemary as a surprise guest. The audience was thrilled. Rosie sang a few songs, and then she introduced Neil. I didn't know it at the time, but that night while I was doing some of my old act, the president of the Shubert was sitting in the audience, and then and there she decided that I was exactly the kind of person she wanted on their board of directors.

She enrolled a mutual friend, Lindy Gold, to draft me, and I readily agreed. I regularly attended board meetings for the next few years, but as a board member I felt like I wasn't really contributing very much. And so, after my fourth year, I went to the chairman of the board, Cheever Tyler, and told him that I was ready to step down.

He looked at me and laughed, saying, "No, you can't. I'm retiring and you're going to take my place. You're stepping up!"

So in the span of less than ten seconds, I went from an exiting low-level board member to chairman of the board for the next five years. And it was during those five years that the Shubert hit a huge fiscal roadblock and almost went under. We had to embark on a major campaign to raise money to pay off the Shubert's mortgage and keep the theater's doors open.

The new president of the Shubert, Caroline Werth, and I had a major problem on our hands. New Haven was facing its own fiscal crisis, and there were not a lot of funds floating around the city. We decided to start by asking Rick Levin, the president of Yale University, for money. Like every university, Yale is a hard sell since they are constantly in the process of raising funds for the school and their own endowment. So, although Yale University was not the most logical choice, I trusted that if we could convey to Rick a sense of what the downtown area would look like with the Shubert dark, I could win him over. Caroline and I went to his office and stressed that if the whole block around the Shubert—which is less than a block from Yale's old campus—was boarded up, wouldn't this convey to prospective Yale students and their parents a bad impression of our city? Rick nodded in agreement and came up with an ingenious idea. Every year, Yale paid $50,000 to sponsor a dance series. So Levin arranged to forward us a half-million dollars as a ten-year advance, and in doing so, he helped to keep the arts alive in New Haven.

Yet that still wasn't enough to pay off our mortgage; we needed more money. Caroline and I went to private foundations, arts councils, even the governor of Connecticut and clearly articulated to each of them how we could not have a viable community without the arts. Over and over again, we emphasized what the Shubert meant on nights that the theater is open in downtown New Haven. We even utilized statistics from restaurants, bars, and parking lots, demonstrating the substantial influx of money that came in on nights the theater was lit. Through our efforts, we conclusively proved the significant economic impact that the Shubert has on the city. Our campaign started working, but the money we received was still not enough. Two days before we were going to have to close, we had yet to reach our goal. Something like panic set in. The theater was in big trouble and despite our efforts, we were still unsure if we were going to be able to keep its doors open.

Ultimately, May 6, 1996, was our D-Day. Would the Shubert survive or die? Caroline and I called a press conference to take place at the theater. I walked out onto a bare stage with a single spotlight; it was all very dramatic. I looked very somber and serious. I started by speaking about the perilous condition that the Shubert was in. Then, I raised my voice and exclaimed, "And I'm here to say we have saved the Shubert!"

The key had been getting rid of the mortgage. The monies that we raised through all the different channels allowed us to pay off the mortgage and become solvent. We had structured a new, five-year plan with the city of New Haven that would let us operate the theater with an annual subsidy. And so, with that announcement, show tunes blasted through the sound system and colorful sets dropped down from the fly space above my head and moved in from the wings. By the time I had finished my speech, the entire stage was dressed. It was pure theater and everybody loved it.

I was chairman of the Shubert board for five years and feel lucky to have had the experience and to have been able to do something that directly impacted the New Haven community in a most favorable way.

Working in the nonprofit world has given me a true appreciation for what people in the arts have to go through to stay afloat and also taught me that despite my childhood dreams, I made the right choice in my life. I was not meant to be a theater owner!

My involvement with the Shubert diversified my life and afforded me the kind of perspective that only association with a worthwhile non-business activity can provide. Regardless of my motivation, my company and I both were enriched by my participation and identification with the Shubert. I'm not suggesting here that you should take up a charitable cause with the idea that it will help you in business. If that's your sole reason, it likely will backfire because your heart really won't be in the effort. Rather, undertake what intrigues you, hopefully with altruistic motives, and regard any business benefits as if they were tax-exempt windfall profits.

34

Pilot Your Life

I'm now sixty-five years old. I've worked hard for a long time and sold a lot of pens, but over the course of my life some things have stayed with me and profoundly affected me. For example, I still remember that when my family moved to Florida in 1948, I saw segregation for the first time. People of color could not drink from the same water fountains as white people, or sit beside them in movie theaters, or ride in the front section of buses. Even when a headline performer like Sammy Davis, Jr. came to Miami to do a show, he was relegated to "colored hotels." I might have been young, and it was many years ago, but the injustice of this type of racism has stayed with me to this day.

In fact, one day in a store when I was ten, my mother tried on a dress. It didn't fit, so she didn't buy it. At the same time, an African-American woman tried on a similar dress, and she was told that she had to buy it because she had tried it on. Ever since then, I've spent a great deal of my time and energy fighting against bigotry. Once I retire, I hope to be able to spend even more time working with some of the charitable organizations with which I am now involved.

Also, I'm happy to report that I have five beautiful grandchildren—Stephanie Santoro, Lauren Shaw, Bryan Shaw, Jacob Shaw, and Yael Shaw. I am looking forward to having more time to spend with them.

In fact, one of my biggest regrets is being so caught up in the business world that I feel I did not get enough time with my own children in their formative years. There were many weeks when I was away two, three, four, or even five days of the week. I really became a weekend father; fortunately, my wife did a phenomenal job of playing both mother and father during the week. However, I cannot stress enough the value of making time for one's own family. When my kids were young and I did come home from a business trip, I would always make a special effort to spend time with each of them, carefully listening and getting up-to-date on everything they had done while I was away. I also tried to schedule my trips around their Little League games and dance recitals.

Speaking of family, there's one last story that is very dear to my heart that I promised at the beginning of this book I would share with you. When I was a young man with a new wife and a baby, I approached my father and asked him to help get me a job at his company as a truck driver. I was flat-out broke and really needed the money. I knew my father was well liked at his company and had a little influence, so I thought the chances of his getting me hired were really good.

He looked over at me and said, "You know, Ron, I think I could get you a job. But if I do, you'll stay at that company, drive a truck every day for the next forty years, collect your pension, and never achieve anything close to what you are capable of."

"But, Dad, it's a good salary—$125 a week. We could really use the—"

"Ron, listen to me. I'm sorry, but I won't do it. I want you to do more. I know you can do better. Trust me, you can do better!"

I was angry with him at the time, but now I see how right he was.

So thanks, Dad. Thank you for not getting me that job and instead urging me on to do more with my life and stretch all the way until I fulfilled my potential. I've come to see how great a gift you gave me on that day. It is this very same gift that I want to give to you, my reader. I hope this book has helped inspire you to stretch a little further and dare to take control of your life and achieve your potential.

Remember, we are all blessed with certain gifts. It is your job in life to find them, exploit them, and, don't forget, along the way try to give something back.

Looking back over my career, there seems to be one great irony that rises above the rest. Even though I have spent the past forty years of my life in the pen business working for others, I have always emphasized to my children and all young people the significance and advantages of working for yourself. There are so many rewards that come from being in business for yourself. There's nothing that can beat the freedom and independence of it. In fact, I'm happy to say that all three of my children and their spouses have their own companies, and I believe they are all better off for it.

In fact, whenever I deliver college commencement addresses, I always ask the graduates to take this little test: "Think for a moment of the five wealthiest people you personally know. I am not talking about Donald Trump or Bill Gates. I am talking about friends and family members."

When they have thought for a few seconds, I go on to say, "Without even knowing any of those five people, I would bet you that at least four of them are in business for themselves." Inevitably, I see the mass of students nodding their heads. It never fails.

In fact, I was told that when one of the fathers of a graduate in the audience heard my speech, he ran home to fulfill his lifelong dream of finally starting his own business. God bless him, and I hope he makes it; yet, even if he doesn't, at least he will know that he tried and will not have to live with the awful specter of "What if?" hanging over his head for the rest of his life.

It has always seemed to me that there are just two kinds of people in this world: Those who want nothing more than a steady job, and those who need to lead, to take chances, to get ahead. And it is those filled with the great entrepreneurial spirit who should and must go into business for themselves.

Though I may have started my career on stage, I've spent the vast majority of my life as a salesperson and a businessman. I love what I do and have no regrets about the choices I've made. I feel very fortunate to have worked with so many great people along the way, and even more fortunate to have each of my setbacks produce something better.

And so, to everyone who's ever had to work for a living or dreamt of being a little more successful, I hope this book has taught you a few things, given you a few laughs, and maybe helped you *Pilot Your Life.*

Index